THE COUNTRY RANGE COOKBOOK

CREATIVE COOKING ON KITCHEN RANGES

CAROL BOWEN

GRUB STREET · LONDON

Published by Grub Street
The Basement, 10 Chivalry Road, London SW11 1HT

This edition published 1997
First published 1993

Photographs by Tim Imrie

British Library Cataloguing in Publication Data
Bowen, Carol
    The country range cookbook: creative cooking on agas, rayburns
    and similar style kitchen ranges. – Rev. and updated ed.
    1. Cookery   2. Stoves
    I. Title
    641.5'8

ISBN 1-898697-80-9

Typeset by BMD Graphics, Hemel Hempstead
Printed and bound in Italy by Vallardi

DEDICATION
For Peter, Lucinda and Charles

ACKNOWLEDGEMENTS

As with all books, there are more people involved in the conception and production of the
publication than the author's name on the jacket. I am indebted to my dear friends Anne Dolamore
and John Davies at Grub Street for their belief and enthusiasm in this project and for their continued
support beyond the normal confines of interested publishers.

Many good, loyal friends, old and new, must be thanked for their encouragement, especially
girlfriends Hilary, Rebecca, Lindy, Ramona, Lorraine and Chris but also men friends like Michael,
John and Peter (who is Headmaster at Sherborne and an avid range-style cook in his valuable spare
time). Their off-the-cuff remarks and chatter about country range cooking has helped me to decide
just what should go into the book and what can be left out.

Superb food photographs throughout have been created by Tim Imrie and Anne Tait, styled by
Anne Dolamore and cooked by myself (who else). I give the former my many thanks.

Continued inspiration has come from a number of sources not least help from food companies
like the Mushroom Grower's Association, British Meat Information Service, Scottish Salmon
Information Service, the Duck Information Service, the Summer Orange Office and Oxo; but
especially from Catherine Blakeley at the Aga Owner's Club (which produces a monthly newsletter
with recipes, special cookware offers and an invaluable agony corner – a must for all range-style
cooks). Special mention must be given to my ever cheerful chums at Country Flowers & Interiors
at Windlesham, Surrey; their creative gifts, flowers and interior design ideas have proved
inspirational for the gift chapter of the book.

Last but not least I must thank my family – husband Peter and children Lucinda and Charles. They
put up with a lot when a book is 'cooking' but always offer support time and time again and even
now, like me, are looking forward to the next tome (perhaps 'Range-style Entertaining?') Happy eating.

CAROL BOWEN

CONTENTS

FOREWORD

For many years I had longed for a country range cooker so was delighted to inherit one when we moved to our present house some ten years ago. Friends and colleagues who had them extolled their virtues by praising the way in which they provided a warm and welcoming kitchen, superb food and an indefinable centre to the whole home.

I liked my Aga's culinary prowess immediately and quickly appreciated the lovely warm atmosphere it gave to our creaky, old house full of packing boxes and little else. But what about all this gushy 'centre' nonsense?

Over the years I have come to know what they meant and nod approvingly when it is ever mentioned as if I am part of some secret society of country range owners and have 'the knowledge'. My range has become the heart of my home. It not only cooks superbly for every occasion from the simple to the sumptuous, and helps with umpteen hated household chores, especially the laundry, but is also where almost everyone congregates to discuss the day's news, troubles and successes. Friends, like magnets, are drawn to its welcoming warm embrace and I frequently have to remind them to move over so that the cook can get into action.

Its not surprising therefore that I treat my range like a time-honoured and trusted friend – it has never let me down and I'm sure it never will. Over the years I have tested hundreds of recipes in it for an ever-growing number of published recipe books, some late into the night when a deadline approached; it has baked a multitude of birthday, anniversary and celebration cakes for my children, husband, family and friends; it has soothed and saved frayed tempers by keeping food appetisingly hot for my ever-delayed husband on the seemingly endless work treadmill; dried flowers, herbs and cooked preserves for much-loved gifts impromptu and planned; and, dare I say it, given me something of a reputation for being a good cook.

I'm not alone in praising its virtues. My children when asked, have said they like how it warms their coats, hats and gloves on a frosty morning; our very old Persian cat Brynny purrs appreciatively at its foot staking her claim for the best seat in the house; my mother hovers nearby with a comfortable cushion enjoying its relaxing, warm glow while she reads a good book (perhaps an Aga Saga?); while my husband, Peter, says its the best machine he knows for quickly drying his swimming gear, golf clothes and sports shoes overnight so that he is well equipped the next day for another session in the quest to keep fit.

I have written many cookery books but have to say this has been the hardest yet at the same time the most enjoyable. Hard because it has been difficult to decide what must be left out – I have wanted to pass on lots of good basic recipes but also many new ideas geared to today's hectic lifestyle. I know that some may buy this book because they haven't a good basic cookbook of their own or, like me, never inherited the book to go with their inherited range. Others will want to add to their recipe library. To make the choice I have taken a long hard look at my friends who own country ranges and hope I have satisfied their needs. So you'll find there are some stylish new recipes using unusual ingredients for my friends Lorraine and Chris who go and try new dishes in lots of super well-known and starred restaurants and cook adventurously at home; some very good, reliable if basic recipes for Gilly who has just bought a new range but finds the foreign cookbook and owner's guide that came with it a bit limited; and as many of my own favourite recipes as space would allow for Hilary who is always asking me to jot down a recipe for a dish she has just tried. The testing, cooking and sampling has been the most rewarding ever. I hope you too will enjoy and savour our combined selection.

CAROL BOWEN

INTRODUCTION

COUNTRY RANGE COOKING – A LIFESTYLE

Country range cookers have become legendary since they were introduced some fifty years ago. They are cookers so brilliantly designed and engineered that they offer a lifetime of virtually trouble-free service and will cook and heat with the options of gas, oil, solid fuel or electricity. They represent not only a way of cooking and heating but an almost indefinable individual style of living that represents warmth, friendliness and a leisurely pace to life.

Such cookers roast, bake, steam, stew, simmer, fry, braise, grill, boil and toast – very impressive when you consider that even with the immense variety of cooking equipment available today, you just can't add to a country range cooker.

All models work in the same way: the burning fuel heats the metal construction of the cooker, which is usually made of cast-iron or pressed steel, for the cooking facility; and in the case of heating and cooking models, this in turn heats water in a surrounding water jacket for the domestic hot water supply and, in many cases, for a limited number of central heating radiators. While some models are simply used purely for cooking, many will supply hot water and some provide central heating. Some can be adapted for central heating with the addition of a boiler unit in gas or oil.

Most of the modern versions of country-style ranges incorporate a damper control that allows you some control over the rate of burning according to the season or average outdoor temperature. So, on the higher winter setting, cookers will not only provide normal cooking temperatures but also a high heat output to keep the kitchen as warm as toast. During the summer months or when temperatures are very mild a reduced setting can be used – this produces only a little heat for warming but the usual expected cooking temperatures in the oven. Some people prefer to turn the range off completely during the warmer months and one new model now has electric elements within its construction for cooking even when not being used for heating. Others have an electric element boost in the main oven to raise the normal main oven temperature for special high temperature cooking.

Most domestic models (for there are many catering versions available) have at least one large oven and one or two smaller, usually cooler, secondary ovens for cooking. In some cases the ovens have a pre-set temperature, in others the main oven can be regulated. This regulation is very real but it is not as accurate nor can it be changed as speedily as with conventional gas or electric cookers. On most, a simple control gives priority heating to the oven and hotplate for high temperature cooking (and most have an oven thermometer to signal when that temperature has been reached). When the control is switched to give priority to water and central heating, the main oven will stay hot enough for slow baking and cooking while the smaller oven can be used for gentle simmering and plate warming.

All manufacturers boast that the cast-iron construction of the country range ensures that heat is radiated evenly within the ovens and that they stay at a good steady and constant temperature, and, because the ovens are sealed, the air stays moist and so drying out and shrinkage of foods like meat are reduced to the very minimum. I have also found that because they retain their heat, you can open doors to peep at foods during cooking without fear of them collapsing! Not slow to respond to modern day demands, many new versions also have catalytic linings to make cleaning that much easier.

Most country ranges are also so much roomier than many ordinary cookers – often you can pile saucepans on top of each other in the oven for cooking, place large and small roasting dishes side by side for even cooking and because of the number of ovens you can move them to and fro to cope with unexpected delays and emergencies.

Although considerably larger than standard appliances, they have also been designed to align in height and depth with modern day stream-lined kitchen units. Needless to say they also come in a whole rainbow of bright and more sombre colours and some can even be fitted with decorative tiling to the front for an integrated or individual look.

Within the whole spectrum of country-style cookers, with and without heating facilities, using any kind of fuel, there are two main types. The first is a heat storage range cooker with ovens and hotplates that are pre-set to fixed temperatures. Within this type there are two-oven and four-oven variations, with each oven pre-set at a different temperature. All the ovens are generally of the same size. The hob top is characterised by two main hotplates – one for fast boiling and a cooler one for simmering.

For use in this book the two-oven type has been assumed to have a Roasting Oven and Simmering/Warming Oven. The four-oven type is assumed to have a Roasting Oven, Baking Oven, Simmering Oven and Warming Oven.

The second type is a heat-storage range cooker with ovens and hotplates that can be varied manually. Generally these are models with just two ovens – the oven at the top for baking and roasting, and a smaller oven underneath for very gentle simmering, warming plates etc. On the top is usually a single hotplate which is graduated in temperature, ranging from boiling at one end to gentle simmering at the other. For use in this book the two-oven type has been assumed to have a main Roasting Oven and secondary Simmering/Warming Oven. The temperature range assumed in the main oven is from 110°C/225°F to 240°C/475°F.

THE CHART ON PAGE 19 SHOWS MANY MANUFACTURER'S MODELS AND WHICH TYPE OF RANGE THEY ARE – TURN TO IT TO LOCATE YOUR OWN MODEL SO THAT YOU CAN FOLLOW THE SPECIFIC RECIPE INSTRUCTIONS FOR THAT TYPE OF COOKER TO ENSURE SUCCESS.

Most ranges come as a standard pack, some need assembling on site, others are delivered as a complete appliance. Some of the more expensive models can be custom-built and are made to order with gas or electric ovens and burners, simmering plates, cast-iron hotplates, deep fryers and barbecue grills. All need to be installed by a qualified fitter, some manufacturers insisting upon their own, for safety. Many have to be vented into a flue or chimney, or in the case of electric models by a small vent pipe. It is wise to have a site visit by the manufacturer and installation engineer before making a final choice.

FEATURES OF A TYPICAL TWO-AND FOUR-OVEN COUNTRY RANGE COOKER

HOTPLATES

The hotplates, whether individual or as a whole plate across the top of the cooker, afford a range of heat from fast boiling down to gentle simmering. Both types give an area that is large enough to hold several pans at the same time. The Boiling Plate, or very hot boiling end of the hotplate, is used when a fierce heat is required. It is primarily used for boiling vegetables, fast frying foods, grilling foods with the use of a cast-iron ridged grill pan, stir-frying, toasting and any high heat culinary cooking method.

The Simmering Plate, or cooler end of the hotplate, in contrast is for much gentler cooking like making sauces, simmering stocks and soups, boiling milk, stewing of hotpots etc. This hotplate can also be used as a griddle for making Scotch pancakes and girdle scones. Needless to say it is possible to use only part of the hotplate by drawing the pan to one side for greater variability of temperature. The hotplates lose heat when their covers are lifted for cooking so when cooking is finished do remember to close them immediately to retain as much heat as possible and to keep running costs low.

On one four-oven country range model there is also an additional Warming Plate which is ideal for keeping foods warm, warming dishes and plates before serving and also makes the perfect hostess hotplate so that guests can serve themselves on occasions like breakfast.

THE OVENS: PRE-SET TEMPERATURE MODELS

TWO-OVEN PRE-SET TEMPERATURE TYPE

In the two-oven pre-set temperature type of country range there is a Roasting Oven and a Simmering Oven. Both ovens are usually of the same size. The Roasting Oven is a very hot oven but can be made into a moderate temperature oven for a short period of time by placing a cold plain shelf above the food being cooked. This effectively reduces the oven temperature for about 30 minutes cooking time. It is generally supplied by the manufacturer of such ranges but can also be purchased separately from country range dealers. The Roasting Oven is used, as its name suggests, for roasting but at the top, where temperatures are very high, it can be used to grill and bake pastries that require high temperatures. The floor makes the ideal medium for frying foods and for baking pastry items that have a bottom crust. In between the two temperature ranges you can bake vegetables, bread, cakes and more.

The Simmering Oven is a gentle oven for slow cooking of meat, casseroles, stews, teabreads, rich fruit cakes etc. In most cases foods have generally started in the Roasting Oven or on the hob before being placed in here to finish cooking. It is an oven for cooking soups, stock, stews, casseroles, rich fruit cakes and everything else that reflects a gentle cooking or simmering action.

FOUR-OVEN PRE-SET TEMPERATURE TYPE

The four-oven pre-set temperature type of country range has the same two ovens as the two-oven type but also an additional two ovens. These are called the Baking Oven and the Plate Warming Oven. The Baking Oven is an oven that has a pre-set moderate temperature ideal for baking cakes, biscuits and some teabreads. Like all the other ovens in the pre-set type the top of the oven is generally hotter than the bottom so positioning of foods is also important and does offer some flexibility and variability in the same oven.

THE HEAT INDICATOR/THERMOSTAT

With pre-set models you can forget about exact temperatures since the ovens have been pre-set for you but it is essential to check that the temperature gauge or indicator shows that it is within the range for ideal cooking. Sometimes the stored heat can mean the oven is a little too high and occasionally, especially when the oven has been used a great deal, it falls below the average range. Don't worry if this level drops back a little as the heat will automatically be restored in a short period of time. The main time to check this indicator is after servicing or after switching back on following a period when the range has been turned off. The control can then be adjusted so that it reaches the optimum average temperature.

THE OVENS: VARIABLE TEMPERATURE MODELS

Within this model type there are many variations but most have one main cooking oven and a secondary oven underneath. The main cooking oven is adjustable to any temperature you require from slow cooking for casseroles and stews to high temperatures for roasting and baking. Often this oven comes with a solid cold metal shelf which can separate the oven into two distinct halves, enabling cooking at two different temperatures at any given time over a short period of time. This main top oven will also grill and fry like the pre-set models by using the floor of the oven and the very top grid shelf. The Warming Oven beneath the main oven is used for cooking those dishes that require extremely delicate or light cooking – meringues for example, depending upon the temperature in the cooking oven above. It is also ideal for warming plates, utensils and cooking and serving dishes.

Even though variable temperature models are designed to be flexible at the touch of a switch or turn of a dial some manufacturers, recognising that they respond a little slower than conventional cookers, have introduced an electric boost to the main oven. This is usually in the form of an electric element and ensures that very hot cooking temperatures are achievable in a short period of time.

STANDARD
AND OPTIONAL EQUIPMENT

Depending upon your manufacturer your country style range may come with shelves, sheets, toasters, saucepans, roasting tins and much more or very little. Certainly all come with the basic grid shelves and most give a roasting tin and cold plain shelf or baking sheet. All these basics can usually be re-ordered (I never think there are enough grid shelves or baking sheets for a typical family's cooking load) from the manufacturer and many also have special cookware, cleaning utensils and special accessories that they recommend and can supply.

KETTLE

Usually more than one size is offered, a small to medium and a very large. All have heavy ground bases to ensure quick even heating of water. I have compared an electric kettle with my range one and the latter had the edge in terms of speedy boiling!

COOKWARE

Cast-iron cookware of the Le Creuset and Agaluxe type are most strongly recommended since they have strong heavy bases that do not warp, can be used on the hob and in the oven, are dishwasher proof and will last for years. Many will also match or contrast beautifully with the colour of your country range. They are heavy and sometimes you will wish that you had the muscles of Popeye but they work fantastically better than anything else I have tried. Having said that, a good range of Pyrex and other freezer-to-oven cookware will also prove invaluable. If you are considering buying new pans then look again for those with a good ground base and consider those with flat lids and metal handle that can be stacked in the oven.

CAST-IRON RIDGED GRILL PAN

Although you can effectively grill at the very top of the Roasting Oven or main oven when set at a high temperature, this piece of cookware offers another alternative method – using the hotplate. The heavy pan with its ridged base is heated, the food is then added and cooked. The result is a striped, grilled or barbecued food that is cooked perfectly on the outside and moist and succulent on the inner. I find that the pan can be heated on the hotplate or in the oven on the oven floor. Press the food firmly onto the hot surface when you add it to get a good contact and the characteristic striping. Use a lid or improvise with a plate to stop splashes if you like.

THE CAKE BAKER

To my knowledge this set of cake-baking equipment is only sold by Aga for use in their two-oven pre-set temperature model of range cookers. The cake baker consists of a deep pan and lid together with a cake rack and three sizes of cake tin, 15, 18 and 20 cm (6, 7 and 8 inch). It is useful for creating a moderate oven atmosphere within the Roasting Oven for baking cakes that require over 45 minutes cooking time. The pan and lid are placed on the floor of the oven to preheat while the cake is being made.
The chosen cake tin is then lined in the usual way and filled with the cake mixture. The cake tin is then placed in the rack making sure it sits level. The rack is then lowered into the pre-heated tin, the lid is placed in position and the cake is then cooked on the floor of the oven. It is a very good piece of equipment for those owners of a two-oven pre-set temperature range who regularly bake cakes and the cake baker pan and lid will double up as a saucepan so are versatile and cost effective.

TOASTING RACK

This is a hinged grill rack rather like the type you use to cook delicate food over the barbecue. Bread of virtually any shape and size is placed between the wires and then cooked on top of the Boiling Plate until golden. The grill is then flipped over for the second side to cook. Use it for making toast, cooking teacakes, cooking toasted sandwiches and toasting crumpets.

OVEN GLOVES

A must with every type of cooker and I strongly recommend that you buy the ones that reach all the way up your arm right to the elbow for safe handling of food right at the back of the oven. I always say that you can recognise a country range cook and check how long she has been cooking this way by the number of brand marks she has up her forearm!

ROASTING TINS

Some manufacturers supply roasting tins for their cooking ranges and the ones that do usually ensure that they will hang from the runners at the side of the oven negating the need for a grid shelf to be used. Many big name household stores now also sell roasting tins that are of a suitable size. Check your oven measurements and go shopping for the best buy. Ideally choose a large one for festive-style catering (when you will cook a very large roast or turkey) and a smaller one for normal family requirements.

CLEANING AND MAINTENANCE

Always follow your specific manufacturer's advice on the care and cleaning of your country range. Special finishes and surfaces may require special cleaning and specific cleaning agents may be recommended for this. In general, cleaning is minimal since most food spills and splashes inside the ovens are quickly burnt away and carbonised. All you will need to do is brush out the debris from the oven floor from time to time. A wire brush will help but again follow specific instructions – you may have an oven with a special lining where wire brushing is certainly not advisable! In nearly all the ranges I have come across oven cleaners are not recommended. Gentle detergents and soft cloths are the safest bets for cleaning the exterior especially if it has a high gloss vitreous enamel surface and certainly choose a non-scratch cleaner for any shiny surface like the shiny hotplate lids.

It makes sense to wipe up spills and splashes as they occur – that way they won't bake on hard and prove troublesome to remove. Milk and fruit juices in particular should be removed immediately since they can stain and discolour and even damage the enamel. For very persistent built-up, baked-on and greasy stains then a soap-filled plastic pad will probably do the trick. Only use metal pads if your manufacturer says it is safe to do so.

Some doors on models can be removed for periodic spring cleaning but this is a wipe and clean operation certainly not a soaking effort – never immerse doors in water since they will invariably be filled with insulating material.

I find it necessary to clean the hotplates themselves occasionally with a wire brush to remove any burnt-on bits of food that have inadvertently popped from the pan. Stray crumbs from the toasting rack also do have a tendency to linger. These are better removed regularly so that pans and cookware maintain a good contact with the hotplate when in use.

The manufacturer's instruction booklet will give any detailed information on cleaning the flues to your particular model if necessary. In general, when this is advised, clean it out once a month using the tools provided. Some fuels, like wood, may require more regular cleaning, more like weekly. Remember however to keep any ashpan emptied regularly to ensure an adequate flow of air to maintain temperature.

LIGHTING, RIDDLING AND REFUELLING OF SOLID FUEL COOKERS

Old hands make light work of these somewhat daunting tasks and practise they say makes perfect. Follow your manufacturer's instructions to the letter. If you are inheriting a solid fuel range and are unsure about these tasks then it is advisable to ask your local agent to take a look first and to check that the range is functioning properly. The engineer will be able to show you the best way of lighting the range as he checks it over. A friendly chat will also often impart years of wisdom and some clever tips or short-cuts.

Since solid fuel ranges need regular riddling and refuelling, check all instructions according to fuel used and frequency of use. When use is heavy, for example during the winter months and when the range is used for cooking and central heating, this may be necessary several times a day and ash removal will be a frequent exercise. Your handbook will give you invaluable advice on specifics. I recommend that everyone in the family over a sensible age should read this so that the chore does not become a very personal one but a family one. One friend has a rota so that it is quite clear whose responsibility it is to make sure there is hot water in the morning and that the oven does not 'go out' through lack of fuel.

SERVICING

To keep your country range running efficiently it is advisable to organise a regular service with a recommended or approved dealer. Never tinker with the working parts yourself or allow an inexperienced D.I.Y. engineer to probe inside the cooker.

COUNTRY RANGE GOLDEN RULES, SPECIAL TIPS AND IN-BUILT BONUSES

GOLDEN RULES

Cook as much as possible in the ovens and make good use of overnight or idling heat. Double-up on quantities and freeze away one meal for a busy time.

- Mop up spills and wipe away splashes as they happen and before they become ingrained or baked-on.

- Look after your range by treating its surface with care – pans, trays and casseroles can all scratch the surface, marring its beauty. Lift carefully from the range rather than drag across.

- Clean regularly following your manufacturer's guide and do organise a regular service with your manufacturer or dealer to ensure years of trouble-free cooking.

- Close doors quickly after inspecting food and keep the hotplate lids firmly down when not cooking to conserve heat and keep running costs to the minimum.

- Don't store tins, equipment and baking trays in the ovens.

- Choose any new equipment you wish to buy with your range very much in mind – look for good quality heavy-based pans with thick ground bases that will give you years of good service. They will generally cost a little more but will last much longer than thinner, poorer quality specimens whose bases warp and buckle easily giving poor contact with the hotplates.

GENERAL

- When boiling the kettle on top of the range, always position the spout so that it faces the hotplate lid – any brown or stubborn splash marks from cooking will then steam away and disappear as if by magic!

- Dry awkward-shaped cooking utensils on the top of the country range – items like graters, piping nozzles, garlic pressers and food processor blades will dry quickly and efficiently without fear of rusting.

- I dry my daughter's much hated but essential school swimming cap over a milk bottle or kitchen towel holder on the top of the range. No fear that it will perish, go mouldy or smell horrible. Do the same with piping bags and toiletry bags with plastic waterproof linings.

- Dry a multitude of flowers over the country range for stylish arrangements and for pot pourri (see page 157).

HOUSEHOLD

- Washable training shoes and plimsoles dry slowly and evenly on top of the country range overnight – much better than the warping effect of too-hot radiators and much faster than the stuff-with-newspaper method.

- Use your country range to dry and air clothes efficiently. I seem to have a constant flow of sports clothes hanging from the front rail but have also constructed a pulley-style wooden rail dryer above for airing linen which I use when the hotplates are not in operation and cooking odours are not troublesome. Wet clothes hung up last thing at night will also be dry by the morning. Do take care however not to cover any ventilation outlets with hanging clothes or cover ventilation slots at the back of the hotplates.

- Some smaller-sized items like socks, tea towels, hand towels and lingerie can, if folded neatly, be dried on the chrome lid of the Simmering Hotplate and produce, after turning once, a 'pressed-like' appearance. A splendid tip for cutting down on loathsome ironing!

- Dry paintings created by an enthusiastic toddler who spreads paint too thickly on top of the range. Far faster than the airing cupboard or normal air drying. Do the same with newspapers that are rain-drenched from being half tucked in and half stuck out of the letterbox.

- If you're trying to sell your house or just want it to smell wonderful then try placing a sprig of rosemary or a bay leaf on the Simmering Plate or cool end of the hotplate and it will fill the kitchen with a beautiful herbal scent.

- If you have a range that uses logs or a house that has open fires then leave a space near to your range for stacking logs and kindling – any damp ones will dry out beautifully for use.

CULINARY

- Do make full use of the Simmering/Warming Oven for keeping food warm before serving, for keeping food warm after serving before seconds are offered and for keeping a meal hot when visitors or family are delayed. (I've found it so much friendlier to say your meal is in the Aga rather than your meal is in the dog!)

- Prepare a casserole in the evening and make good use of overnight heat in the Simmering or Warming Oven for cooking. Cool quickly the next morning then chill until required in the refrigerator or freezer. Reheat in the top of the oven or on the top of the range but make sure the casserole cooks at boiling point for 10 minutes before serving.

- Thaw casseroles on top of the range or in the Warming Oven but cook immediately after thawing this way since it will have already started to heat through.

- Some of the more popular two-oven country range cookers come with a cold plain shelf so that you can cook at moderate temperatures in the Roasting Oven – do use this as an extra shelf when required but don't store in the oven.

- Make full use of the early summer bounty of fresh herbs by drying some above the range for winter use (see page 156).

- Use the top of the range to thaw and defrost foods from the freezer quickly and efficiently. This is a wizard with baked cakes, bread and biscuits. Do ensure that all meat, fish and poultry are thoroughly thawed right through to their centres before cooking (for best results start on the range then move to the work surface or refrigerator for the remainder of the time).

- Use the range to soften, melt or warm foods for cooking. Soften butter and sugar for easy creaming; heat jam, honey or marmalade for easy spreading; melt chocolate for spreading or using in recipes by placing in a bowl on top of the range; and warm ingredients for bread making to ensure success.

- Cook meat and bones for family pets by bringing to the boil on the Boiling Plate then transferring to the Simmering or Warming Oven until tender.

- Dry bacon rinds in a tin in the Simmering Oven until crisp for feeding to the birds and citrus rinds for adding to pot pourri or casseroles (a piece of orange in a beef casserole imparts a wonderful flavour).

- Dry bread for oil-free croûtons and for dried breadcrumbs in the Simmering Oven until crisp. Use croûtons to top soup and salads and use breadcrumbs in stuffings and savoury coatings.

- Toast nuts, seeds and coconut quickly in the Roasting Oven to an even golden colour for use in nibbles, desserts and baking.

- Warm citrus fruits on top of the range for a good 10-15 minutes before squeezing – this way you will get the maximum yield from a fruit.

- I rarely drink a cup of coffee or tea when it is piping hot, something always crops up to draw me away. I have learnt however that if I place it on top of the range it stays wonderfully hot for what seems like hours so that I can return and enjoy it.

- Cereals and biscuits that have lost their crispness can be revived by heating in the Warming Oven.

- Use the Warming Oven for warming plates but also use it to rest meats before carving, keeping sauces and gravies warm, for keeping meals for latecomers (covered with foil) and for warming tins and equipment for yeast-style baking.

BEFORE YOU BEGIN

- Note that unless otherwise stated, flour is of the plain variety, water is cold, eggs are size 3, sugar is granulated and all spoon quantities are measured level.

- Both metric and Imperial measures are given. Metric measurements may vary from one entry to another within the book for recipe success. It is essential to follow one set of quantities either metric or Imperial since they have not been tested to be interchangeable.

- EGGS – THE GOVERNMENT RECOMMENDS THAT EGGS SHOULD NOT BE CONSUMED RAW, AND PEOPLE MOST AT RISK, SUCH AS CHILDREN, OLD PEOPLE, INVALIDS AND PREGNANT WOMEN, SHOULD NOT EAT THEM LIGHTLY COOKED. THIS BOOK INCLUDES SOME RECIPES WITH RAW AND LIGHTLY COOKED EGGS AND SHOULD NOT BE EATEN

BY THE ABOVE CATEGORIES. ONCE PREPARED, THESE DISHES SHOULD BE KEPT REFRIGERATED AND USED PROMPTLY.

- The cooking instructions within the recipes have been devised and tested for many different makes and types of country range cookers. Check your model against the list given below, then follow the appropriate symbol for recipe success.

MAKE OF OVEN	Follow 2 oven Pre-Set Model Instructions	Follow 4 oven Pre-Set Model Instructions	Follow Thermodial Model Instructions
AGA			
Electric 2 Oven	●		
Electric 4 Oven		●	
Gas-Fired 2 Oven	●		
Gas-Fired 4 Oven		●	
Oil-Fired 2 Oven	●		
Oil-Fired 4 Oven		●	
Solid-Fuel 2 Oven	●		
Solid-Fuel 4 Oven		●	
BOSKY			
Bosky 10			●
Bosky 20			●
Bosky 60			●
Bosky 90			●
COUNTRY COOKERS			
Nobel Gas	●		
Nobel Oil	●		
ESSE			
Sovereign			●
Sovereign Select			●
Premier			●
Doric			●
FRANCO BELGE			
La Premiere GT			●
La Premiere De Luxe			●
La Gretalux AL			●
RAYBURN			
Royal			●
Nouvelle			●
Regent			●
STANLEY			
Traditional Cooker/Boiler			●
Super Star			●

MAKE OF OVEN (Continued)	Follow 2 oven Pre-Set Model Instructions	Follow 4 oven Pre-Set Model Instructions	Follow Thermodial Model Instructions
WAMSLER			
K51V, K61, K61VC, K61U,			
K71V, K81V			●
K125V			●
K147V			●
K170V			●
K178V			●
K101/Country			●
YORKPARK LTD Viscount Central Heating Cooker			●
Duchess Central Heating Cooker			●

SYMBOLS

2 Refers to two-oven thermostatically controlled country ranges with ovens and hotplates that are pre-set to fixed temperatures.

4 Refers to four-oven thermostatically controlled country ranges with ovens and hotplates that are pre-set to fixed temperatures.

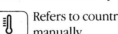 Refers to country ranges where the ovens and hotplates can be varied manually.

It is important to remember that not only do different models of country range cookers differ appreciably but also individual cookers of the same type vary from one to another. In part this is due to the fuel type chosen but cooker location, flue, usage whether heavy and frequent or light and variable and weather conditions all mean that no two cookers are ever the same. It is therefore suggested that the cook errs on the side of safety with the cooking times to begin with, until familiar with the times recommended and how they compare to actual ones experienced.

SOUPS, STARTERS, PARTY NIBBLES AND SNACKS

THE STOCKPOT

I used to cringe when I came to the words "take ¼ pint home-made stock" in my pre-range cooker days. I knew that home-made stock tasted infinitely better than commercial offerings but making it on a regular basis seemed such a chore. Now I always have a selection of stocks ready at hand for cooking be they beef, vegetable, chicken or fish – and I freeze away a good quantity to cope with busy cooking periods like Christmas. The secret is to let the range do the work while you sleep!

LIGHT BEEF, LAMB, VEAL, CHICKEN OR GAME STOCK

Place as many large beef, lamb or veal bones or the carcasses of a chicken, duck or game bird into the largest pan or stockpot you have. Cover with water and add a selection of flavouring vegetables like quartered onions, halved carrots and diced celery sticks. Add a bouquet garni and a few whole peppercorns. Bring to the boil and simmer for 10 minutes.

2 **4** 2 OVEN RANGE AND 4 OVEN RANGE: Cover tightly with the pan lid. Transfer to the floor of the Simmering Oven and cook overnight or for at least 8 hours. Remove from the oven, skim off any excess fat and strain to use.

THERMODIAL-CONTROLLED RANGE: Cover tightly with the pan lid. Transfer to the oven set at 150°C/300°F and cook for 3-4 hours. Remove from the oven, skim off any excess fat and strain to use. If you wish to cook the stock overnight then cook in the oven for at least the first hour then transfer to the Simmering/Warming Oven overnight or for at least 8 hours. Remove from the oven, skim off any excess fat and strain to use.

VARIATION

Rich Beef, Lamb or Veal Stock: Prepare and cook as above but brown the bones in a hot oven before cooking, about 45 minutes.

VEGETABLE STOCK

Place a good selection of chopped vegetables in a large pan or stockpot (good ones include carrots, celery, onions, a few green vegetables, leeks and a little swede or turnip) with water to cover. Add a bouquet garni and a few whole peppercorns. Bring to the boil, cover and allow to simmer for 10 minutes.

 2 OVEN RANGE AND 4 OVEN RANGE: Transfer to the floor of the Simmering Oven and cook for 3 hours. Strain to use.

 THERMODIAL-CONTROLLED RANGE: Transfer to the oven set at 150°C/300°F and cook for about 2-2½ hours. Strain to use.

FISH STOCK

Place white fish bones, heads and trimmings in the pan or stockpot. Cover with water and add a selection of flavouring vegetables like onions, leeks and celery. Add a bouquet garni and a few whole peppercorns. Bring to the boil, cover and allow to simmer for 10 minutes. Skim well.

 2 OVEN RANGE AND 4 OVEN RANGE: Transfer to the floor of the Simmering Oven and cook for 1 hour. Strain to use.

 THERMODIAL-CONTROLLED RANGE: Transfer to the oven set at 150°C/300°F and cook for about 1 hour. Strain to use.

STORAGE AND KEEPING STOCK FRESH

- Beef stocks keep well in the refrigerator for up to 1 week but fish and vegetable stocks should be used within 3 days.

- Always store stock in the refrigerator and bring to the boil for 5 minutes every other day to ensure it stays fresh.

- Beef, Chicken and Vegetable stocks can be frozen and will keep up to 3 months but Fish stocks should only be frozen for up to 2 months.

SUMMER ORANGE VICHYSSOISE

Here is the perfect soup for summer entertaining. It is refreshing and light served chilled when the sun is sizzling, yet is just as good hot when the weather is contrary.

SERVES 4

4 small or 2 large leeks, sliced

1 onion, sliced

2 cloves garlic, crushed

15 g (½ oz) butter or
1 tablespoon olive oil

900 ml (1½ pints) good
chicken stock

225 g (8 oz) potato, peeled
and sliced

salt and pepper

4 oranges

4 tablespoons crème fraîche or
thick natural yogurt

To garnish

4 teaspoons black lumpfish roe

fresh chives

2 **4** **🌡** 2 OVEN RANGE, 4 OVEN RANGE, THERMODIAL-CONTROLLED RANGE: Place the leeks in a pan with the onion, garlic and butter or olive oil. Fry gently for about 10 minutes until softened.

Add the stock, potato and salt and pepper to taste. Bring to the boil, cover and simmer gently until the vegetables are soft, about 20 minutes. Alternatively, bring to the boil then cook on the floor of the Simmering or Baking Oven until soft, about 20-30 minutes.

Meanwhile set aside ½ orange for the garnish. Grate the zest from 1 orange and add to the vegetable mixture. Extract the juice from the oranges and add three-quarters of it to the soup mixture. Allow to cool slightly then purée in a blender or food processor until smooth. Stir in the remaining orange juice and leave to cool.

When cool, stir in the crème fraîche or yogurt and taste and adjust the seasoning if necessary. Chill thoroughly or reheat gently without boiling for serving.

Serve the soup in bowls garnished with two half slices of orange cut from the reserved ½ orange, a spoonful of lumpfish roe and a few chives.

CARROT SOUP WITH CURRIED HORSERADISH CREAM

SERVES 4

1 kg (2¼ lb) carrots

1 litre (1¾ pints) water

600 ml (1 pint) chicken or vegetable stock

2½ cm (1 inch) piece root ginger, peeled and grated

1 tablespoon orange juice

salt and pepper

Cream

150 ml (¼ pint) double cream

scant ½ teaspoon curry powder

1 teaspoon creamed horseradish

snipped chives or coriander sprigs, to garnish

This is a delicious carrot soup with overtones of ginger topped with floating spoonfuls of cream flavoured with curry powder and creamed horseradish. Bottled creamed horseradish and horseradish sauce varies enormously in strength so do check before adding to the cream that you have the type you like for flavour. The cream topping is also very good with lentil-style soups.

2 4 🌡 2 OVEN RANGE, 4 OVEN RANGE, THERMODIAL-CONTROLLED RANGE: Cut the carrots into bite-sized pieces and place in a large heavy-based pan with the water. Bring to the boil then simmer for 20 minutes, or until very tender. Drain thoroughly, reserving 300 ml (½ pint) of the cooking liquid.

Place the carrots, reserved cooking liquid and stock in a food processor or blender and purée until smooth. Return to the pan, add the ginger, orange juice and salt and pepper to taste, mixing well. Bring to the boil then simmer for 10 minutes.

Meanwhile to make the cream, place the cream, curry powder and creamed horseradish in a bowl and whip until the mixture stands in soft peaks.

To serve, ladle the soup into individual soup bowls and top each with a floating spoonful of the prepared cream. Garnish with snipped chives or sprigs of fresh coriander and serve.

CANNELLINI AND BACON SOUP

SERVES 6

225 g (8 oz) dried cannellini or other white beans, soaked overnight

350 g (12 oz) lean back bacon, rinded and chopped

1 large onion, chopped

3 cloves garlic, crushed

900 ml (1½ pints) beef or vegetable stock

350 g (12 oz) carrots, thinly sliced

1 large green pepper, cored, seeded and sliced into strips

1 large red pepper, cored, seeded and sliced into strips

225 g (8 oz) cooked smoked ham, cut into small cubes

1 teaspoon snipped chives

¼ teaspoon ground cumin

1 teaspoon chopped fresh thyme

pinch of dark brown sugar

A hearty bean soup to serve when appetites are large or when a main-course style soup is required for lunch-time eating.

2 **4** 🌡 2 OVEN RANGE, 4 OVEN RANGE, THERMODIAL-CONTROLLED RANGE: Drain the beans and rinse well. Place in a large heavy-based pan with enough water to cover, bring to the boil then simmer for 30 minutes or until almost tender. Drain well, reserving the cooking liquid.

Meanwhile, place the bacon in another heavy-based pan and cook until the bacon is crisp. Add the onion and garlic and cook until softened, stirring occasionally.

Add the stock, carrots, peppers, ham, chives, cumin, thyme and sugar, mixing well. Stir in the cooked beans and enough of the reserved cooking liquid to make a soup with a thick and hearty consistency. Bring to the boil then simmer for about 30 minutes or until the vegetables are tender and the beans are fully cooked and soft but not fallen, adding a little more of the reserved liquid if necessary. Serve hot.

LEEK AND STILTON SOUP

SERVES 4

50 g (2 oz) butter

225 g (8 oz) leeks, chopped

1 onion, peeled and chopped

600 ml (1 pint) vegetable stock

150 ml (¼ pint) milk

50 g (2 oz) Stilton cheese, crumbled

salt and pepper

finely chopped spring onions and croûtons, to garnish

Just the soup to make after Christmas when the Stilton is beyond presentation but a good few bits are still worth eating.

2 **4** **🌡** 2 OVEN RANGE, 4 OVEN RANGE, THERMODIAL-CONTROLLED RANGE: Melt the butter in a large heavy-based pan, add the leeks and onion and cook gently until soft, stirring occasionally, about 10 minutes. (This can be done on the floor of the oven if you like).

Add the stock and milk, bring to the boil then simmer, uncovered, for 10 minutes. Remove from the heat and allow to cool until hand hot.

Pour the mixture into a blender or food processor, add the Stilton and purée until smooth.

Return to the pan, add salt and pepper to taste and reheat gently until hot. Serve in warmed soup bowls, garnished with the spring onions and croûtons.

CIABATTA PIZZA

SERVES 2

1 ciabatta loaf

1 x 190 g (6½ oz) jar pesto sauce

150 g (5 oz) Cheddar cheese, grated

1 red onion, sliced

225 g (8 oz) tomatoes, sliced

100 g (4 oz) Mozzarella cheese, sliced

fresh basil sprigs

Italian ciabatta bread makes the perfect base for a pizza-style dish. I have experimented many times with the toppings and the combinations are virtually endless. For example, instead of using pesto in the recipe below use a thick tomato and onion sauce or a spread made with sun-dried tomatoes, herbs and oil and replace the red onions with chopped spring onions.

Split the ciabatta loaf in half lengthways. Spread the pesto sauce over both of the cut surfaces of the loaf evenly. Top with the grated Cheddar cheese, onion separated into rings, tomatoes and finally the sliced Mozarella. Sprinkle with the basil. Place on a large baking sheet.

2 **4** 2 OVEN RANGE AND 4 OVEN RANGE: Place the baking sheet on the grid shelf on the highest set of runners in the Roasting Oven and cook for 10-15 minutes or until browned, crisp and the cheese is bubbling.

🌡 THERMODIAL-CONTROLLED RANGE: Cook in the oven set at 220-230°C/425-450°F for 10-15 minutes or until browned, crisp and the cheese is bubbling.

TARAMASALATA AND HUMMUS FILO CUPS

MAKES ABOUT 24

1 x 225 g (8 oz) packet frozen filo pastry, thawed

75 g (3 oz) butter, melted

75 g (3 oz) taramasalata

75 g (3 oz) hummus

1 small red pepper, cored, seeded and chopped

6 spring onions, finely chopped

 These are delicious bite-sized crisp cups of filo pastry filled with a savoury mixture of taramasalata and hummus that are perfect for festive entertaining.

Cut the filo pastry sheets into 6 cm (2½ inch) squares – you should get about 48. Brush two squares with melted butter and place one square on top of the other at a slight angle, then place in small bun trays. Repeat with the remaining filo pastry squares brushing each with melted butter before assembling in the trays.

 2 OVEN RANGE AND 4 OVEN RANGE: Cook the trays in the Roasting Oven with the grid shelf on the lowest set of runners for about 5 minutes or until the pastry cups are crisp and golden.

THERMODIAL-CONTROLLED RANGE: Cook the trays in the oven set at 190°C/375°F for about 5 minutes or until the pastry cups are crisp and golden.

Remove from the oven, allow to cool then transfer to a wire rack to cool completely. Store in an airtight tin until required but no longer than 2-3 days.

Place the taramasalata and hummus in separate bowls. Add half of the chopped pepper and spring onions to each, mixing well.

To serve, spoon the mixtures individually into the crisp filo cups. Do not fill for longer than 2-3 hours before serving.

CRISPY POTATO SKINS

SERVES 6

8 x 225 g (8 oz) baking potatoes

olive oil

ground paprika, for sprinkling

sea salt, for sprinkling

soured cream, to serve

 At one of our favourite American restaurants they serve crisp, baked potato skins as a starter with soured cream and other dips. They are totally irresistible and very moreish! Sadly for my waistline, I have devised how to make these at home. Try them, but you have been warned, you can't stop at just one!

Scrub the potatoes, pat dry then rub the skins with olive oil. Prick with a fork to prevent bursting.

 2 OVEN RANGE AND 4 OVEN RANGE: Cook in the Roasting Oven, with the grid shelf on the third set of runners, for about 1-1¼ hours until tender.

THERMODIAL-CONTROLLED RANGE: Cook in the oven set at 220°C/425°F for about 1-1¼ hours or until tender.

Remove from the oven and allow the potatoes to cool so that they can be easily handled. Halve lengthwise and scoop out the flesh, leaving a 5 mm (¼ inch) shell. Use the cooked potato for another dish. Cut each half shell of potato lengthwise into 2 or 3 wedges and arrange on a baking sheet. Brush with oil, sprinkle with a little paprika and sea salt to taste. Return to the oven and cook for a further 20-25 minutes or until crisp and golden brown.

Serve hot with the soured cream.

CHICKEN WINGS WITH PARMESAN AND MUSTARD

MAKES 20

100 g (4 oz) butter

2 tablespoons Dijon mustard

large pinch of cayenne pepper

100 g (4 oz) fine dried breadcrumbs

50 g (2 oz) freshly grated Parmesan

1 teaspoon ground cumin

salt and pepper

20 chicken wings, wing tips cut off and discarded and the wings halved at the joint

 Here is a recipe for finger-style food that is ideal to serve, with napkins, at a drinks party or informal gathering. The chicken wings are tasty enough to be served alone but could be accompanied by a tomato-based dip if you prefer.

Place the butter in a pan and melt over a gentle heat. Allow to cool slightly then whisk in the mustard and cayenne pepper. Transfer to a shallow dish.

In another shallow dish mix the breadcrumbs with the Parmesan, cumin and salt and pepper to taste.

Dip the chicken wings, a few at a time, into the butter mixture to coat, then into the Parmesan mixture to coat evenly. Place on a baking sheet so that they do not touch one another.

2 4 2 OVEN RANGE AND 4 OVEN RANGE: Cook in the Roasting Oven with the grid shelf on the lowest set of runners for 30 minutes, turning over once.

 THERMODIAL-CONTROLLED RANGE: Cook in the bottom of the oven set at 220°C/425°F for 30 minutes, turning over once.

Serve warm or cold.

PARMESAN AND HAM PUFFS

MAKES 8

3 tablespoons milk

3 tablespoons water

50 g (2 oz) unsalted butter

¼ teaspoon salt

50 g (2 oz) plain flour

2 large eggs (size 1 or 2)

100 g (4 oz) freshly grated Parmesan

50 g (2 oz) cooked ham, finely chopped

2 teaspoons snipped chives

Deliciously crisp yet fluffy mouthfuls which are perfect to serve with pre-dinner drinks. They are however good accompaniments to soups, meats and poultry. They can be made a day ahead if stored in an airtight tin but should be refreshed in a hot oven before serving.

Place the milk, water and butter in a heavy-based pan and heat gently until the butter melts. Bring to the boil, remove from the heat and add the salt and flour all at once. Beat well with a wooden spoon until the mixture leaves the sides of the pan clean and forms a ball.

Whisk in the eggs, one at a time, whisking very well after each addition. Stir in the Parmesan, ham and chives, mixing well.

Spoon or pipe the mixture into 8 mounds on a lightly greased baking sheet, allowing plenty of room for the puffs to spread and rise.

2 **4** 2 OVEN RANGE AND 4 OVEN RANGE: Bake in the Roasting Oven with the grid shelf on the lowest set of runners for about 20 minutes or until light golden brown. Transfer to the Simmering Oven for a further 15 minutes until very crisp.

THERMODIAL-CONTROLLED RANGE: Bake in the top of the oven set at 200°C/400°F for about 20 minutes or until golden brown. Transfer to the Simmering/Warming Oven for a further 15 minutes until very crisp.

VEAL AND PORK TERRINE

SERVES 8

450 g (1 lb) lean belly of pork, rind removed and minced

450 g (1 lb) pie veal, minced

225 g (8 oz) smoked streaky bacon, rinded and minced

150 ml (¼ pint) red wine or sherry

2 cloves garlic, crushed

2 teaspoons chopped fresh thyme

1 teaspoon chopped fresh rosemary

3 tablespoons dried white breadcrumbs

½ teaspoon ground nutmeg

salt and pepper

2 tablespoons brandy

3 bay leaves

a few juniper berries

I've made this pâté countless times using various proportions of veal, pork and bacon. The veal can be replaced with boned raw game like pheasant, rabbit or hare if you prefer. Serve straight from the dish with interesting but homely bread.

Mix the pork with the veal, bacon and wine or sherry until well blended. Add the garlic, thyme, rosemary, breadcrumbs, nutmeg and salt and pepper to taste. Add the brandy if using and mix well. Cover and leave to stand in a cool place overnight or for at least 8 hours for the flavours to develop.

Spoon into a well-greased 1 kg (2 lb) loaf tin or terrine and level the surface. Place the bay leaves and a few juniper berries on top in an attractive pattern. Cover with foil and stand in a bain marie or small roasting tin, half-filled with boiling water.

2 2 OVEN RANGE: Cook in the Roasting Oven with the grid shelf placed on the oven floor and the cold plain shelf on the second set of runners, for about 1¾ hours, or until the juices run clear.

4 4 OVEN RANGE: Hang the bain marie or roasting tin on the third set of runners in the Baking Oven and cook for about 1¾-2 hours, or until the juices run clear.

THERMODIAL-CONTROLLED RANGE: Cook in the oven set at 160°C/325°F for about 1½-1¾ hours, or until the juices run clear.

Remove from the oven, cool, weight and chill for at least 8 hours before serving. Again best left overnight to chill for the flavours to develop.

PROVENCAL AUBERGINES

SERVES 4

4 small aubergines

½ x 50 g (2 oz) can anchovy fillets

1 clove garlic, crushed

1 tablespoon chopped fresh parsley

1 tablespoon chopped fresh basil

½ small red onion, very finely chopped

4 tablespoons virgin olive oil

2 large 'beef' tomatoes, thinly sliced

pepper

 This is an aromatic dish of aubergines, spiked with tomatoes, garlic and puréed anchovies, basted with a herby olive oil then baked to make a splendid starter or light lunch dish. It can be eaten hot but is much better served cold with warm crusty bread to mop up the juices.

Halve the aubergines lengthwise. Place cut side down on a board and make a few deep cuts along their length almost through to the base. Purée the anchovy fillets, garlic, parsley, basil, onion and half of the olive oil in a blender to make a paste then spread over the aubergines deep into the slits. Insert the tomato slices into the slits as far as possible. Place the aubergines, flat sides down, in a greased baking dish. Drizzle with the remaining oil and season generously with pepper.

2 2 OVEN RANGE: Cook in the Roasting Oven with the grid shelf on the oven floor and the cold plain shelf on the second set of runners until the aubergines are cooked and tender, about 40-45 minutes.

4 4 OVEN RANGE: Cook in the Baking Oven on the third set of runners until the aubergines are cooked and tender, about 45 minutes.

THERMODIAL-CONTROLLED RANGE: Cook in the oven set at 180°C/350°F until the aubergines are cooked and tender, about 40-45 minutes.

BAKED CRAB OR LOBSTER-STUFFED AVOCADOS

SERVES 4

2 large, ripe avocados

lemon juice

225 g (8 oz) crab meat or lobster meat

4 tablespoons mayonnaise

2 spring onions, finely chopped

1 tablespoon red wine vinegar

salt and cayenne pepper

1 egg white

 Cook this doubly delicious starter just before serving (although you can make the topping in advance up to folding in the egg whites). Serve with crisp Melba toast or crackers if you prefer.

Halve the avocados and remove the stones. Rub the cut surfaces with lemon juice to prevent them turning brown and set aside.

Flake the crab or lobster meat or dice into small chunks and mix with the mayonnaise, spring onions and vinegar. Season to taste with salt and cayenne pepper. Whisk the egg white until it stands in stiff peaks and fold into the fish mixture with a metal spoon.

Place the avocado halves in a shallow baking dish into which they will fit snugly, to prevent them from falling over. Pile the fish mixture into the hollows of the avocado halves.

2 2 OVEN RANGE: Cook in the Roasting Oven with the grid shelf on the bottom set of runners and the cold solid shelf above for about 20 minutes or until the filling is puffed and golden brown and the avocados are piping hot.

4 4 OVEN RANGE: Cook in the Baking Oven with the grid shelf on the highest set of runners for about 20-25 minutes or until the filling is puffed and golden brown and the avocados are piping hot.

⬚ THERMODIAL-CONTROLLED RANGE: Cook in the oven set at 180°C/350°F for 20-25 minutes or until the filling is puffed and golden brown and the avocados are piping hot.

Transfer to serving dishes and serve at once.

BAKED CHEVRE ON A LEAFY BED

SERVES 4

4 thin slices of country-style bread (sourdough for example)

---

4 small goat's cheeses

---

4 tablespoons olive oil

---

1 clove garlic, crushed (optional)

---

mixed salad leaves, to serve (lamb's lettuce, frisée, rocket, endive and radicchio, for example)

---

4 tablespoons prepared French dressing, with herbs

Some of the very simplest ideas for a starter work best and this is no exception – individual portions of goat's cheese are oven baked on a piece of bread then served on a leafy bed of seasonal salad leaves drizzled with a herby dressing.

Place the slices of bread on a baking tray and top each with a whole small goat's cheese. Mix the oil with the garlic if used then drizzle over the cheese and bread.

2 **4** 2 OVEN RANGE AND 4 OVEN RANGE: Cook in the Roasting Oven for about 10-15 minutes or until the cheese bubbles and browns on top.

⬚ THERMODIAL-CONTROLLED RANGE: Cook in the oven set at 200°C/400°F for about 10-15 minutes or until the cheese bubbles and browns on top.

Meanwhile, toss the salad leaves in the dressing and divide between four individual serving plates. Top each with a baked chevre and serve at once.

OPPOSITE:
Carrot Soup with Curried Horseradish Cream

PRAWN AND GARLIC BROCHETTES

SERVES 2
(as a main course)
4 (as a starter)

about 2 heads of garlic,
containing a total of 18 cloves

1 tablespoon dill seeds

2 tablespoons finely chopped
fresh dill

2 tablespoons lemon juice

pinch of cayenne pepper

150 ml (¼ pint) vegetable oil

18 large Mediterranean
prawns, cooked or raw with
shells removed

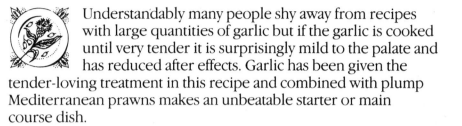

Understandably many people shy away from recipes with large quantities of garlic but if the garlic is cooked until very tender it is surprisingly mild to the palate and has reduced after effects. Garlic has been given the tender-loving treatment in this recipe and combined with plump Mediterranean prawns makes an unbeatable starter or main course dish.

Place the unpeeled garlic heads in a pan with enough water to cover, bring to the boil and cook for 15-20 minutes or until the garlic is tender but not soft. Drain and carefully peel away the skin leaving the garlic cloves whole.

Whisk the dill seeds with the chopped fresh dill, lemon juice and cayenne pepper. Gradually whisk in the oil, in a steady stream, to make a thick and creamy marinade.

Thread the prawns and garlic cloves onto 4 wooden skewers (that have been soaked in warm water for 1 hour). Place in a shallow dish and pour over the prepared marinade. Cover and leave to marinate for 3 hours, turning occasionally.

To cook, drain the skewers from the marinade and place on a baking sheet.

2 4 2 OVEN RANGE AND 4 OVEN RANGE: Cook in the Roasting Oven with the grid shelf on the third set of runners until the prawns are cooked through and hot. Allow about 4-5 minutes for prawns that have already been cooked and about 6-7 minutes for prawns that are raw.

THERMODIAL-CONTROLLED RANGE: Cook in the top of the oven set at 220°C/425°F until the prawns are cooked through and hot. Allow about 4-5 minutes for prawns that have already been cooked and about 6-7 minutes for prawns that are raw.

OPPOSITE:
Ciabatta Pizzas

QUARTERDECKS SMOKED FISH PATE

SERVES 4

100 g (4 oz) unsalted butter

1 shallot, finely chopped

225 g (8 oz) smoked mackerel or trout fillets, skinned and boned weight

100 g (4 oz) cream cheese

1 teaspoon Cognac

½ teaspoon Worcestershire sauce

2 tablespoons lemon juice

crisp crackers, to serve

 The inspiration for this recipe came from a restaurant called Quarterdecks in Massachusetts where seafood is something of a speciality. The original was made with smoked bluefish. Since bluefish, a freshwater fish caught off the Atlantic coast of America, and in the Mediterranean, is seldom found here, my version uses smoked mackerel or trout.

2 4 🌡 2 OVEN RANGE, 4 OVEN RANGE, THERMODIAL-CONTROLLED RANGE: Place the butter and shallot in a small pan and cook until softened, about 5 minutes. Allow to cool.

Place the onion and butter mixture in a food processor or blender with the smoked fish, cream cheese, Cognac, Worcestershire sauce and lemon juice and purée until smooth. Spoon into a small bowl, cover and chill until required.

Serve with crisp crackers.

MUSHROOM, BROCCOLI AND BEAN STIR-FRY

SERVES 4

2 tablespoons oil

175 g (6 oz) broccoli, stalks sliced and heads divided into small florets

100 g (4 oz) fresh baby or dwarf corn

1 large leek, chopped

1 yellow pepper, cored, seeded and cut into cubes

350 g (12 oz) closed cup mushrooms, quartered

3 tablespoons light soy sauce

1 tablespoon clear honey

2 teaspoons ground ginger

1 x 400 g (14 oz) can cannellini beans, drained

 Mushrooms are a good source of minerals and B vitamins aside from their most positive attributes of being low in calories, low in fat and cholesterol free! Here they are cooked in minutes with broccoli, baby corn, leeks and peppers for an instant hot starter, snack or light lunch dish.

2 4 🌡 2 OVEN RANGE, 4 OVEN RANGE, THERMODIAL-CONTROLLED RANGE: Heat the oil in a large heavy-based frying pan on the Boiling Plate. Add the broccoli stalks and cook for 2 minutes. Stir in the broccoli florets and baby corn and cook for a further 2 minutes.

Stir in the leek, pepper and mushrooms and cook for 2 minutes. Stir in the soy sauce, honey, ginger and cannellini beans, mixing well. Cover and cook for 3 minutes, stirring frequently until hot and cooked through. Serve at once.

BREAKFASTS AND BRUNCHES

THE BIG BREAKFAST

Rarely do we, as a nation, have a big cooked breakfast on a daily basis but we rather like the idea for a weekend treat. I often cook a hearty selection of sausages, bacon, eggs, mushrooms, tomatoes, and sometimes fried bread when guests stay since, like me, I assume they enjoy a big breakfast away from home. Make your selection from the ingredients below then cook in the ideal position in the range for the recommended times, putting the longest cooking item in first and adding the others in descending order of cooking times for perfect end results.

BACON: Cook in the top of the Roasting Oven or the oven set at about 200-220°C/400-425°F. Place the bacon on a rack in a roasting pan. This produces a 'grilled'-style rasher. Alternatively, place the bacon in the bottom of a greased roasting pan and place on the oven floor – this will produce a 'fried'-style rasher. Allow about 3-4 minutes each side for medium thickness bacon, turning over halfway through the cooking time.

SAUSAGES: Cook in the top of the Roasting Oven or the oven set at about 200-220°C/400-425°F. Place the sausages on a rack in a roasting pan. Cook for about 20 minutes for standard thickness sausages, turning halfway through the cooking time. Chipolata sausages will take about 12-15 minutes.

TOMATOES: Halve tomatoes and place on the rack in the roasting tin or place directly onto the roasting tin base. Cook in the Roasting Oven or the oven set at 200-220°C/400-425°F for about 10-15 minutes, depending upon size, until tender. Dot with a little butter and season with salt and pepper before cooking if you like.

EGGS: Break eggs onto the base of the greased roasting tin. Cook on the floor of the Roasting Oven or oven set at 200-220°C/400-425°F for about 2-3 minutes.

MUSHROOMS: Place whole or halved mushrooms on the rack in the roasting tin and dot with a little butter. Cook in the top of the Roasting Oven or oven set at 200-220°C/400-425°F for about 5 minutes, turning over once halfway through the cooking time.

FRIED BREAD: Spread the bread with a little butter or bacon fat and place directly on the bottom of a roasting tin. Cook on the floor of the Roasting Oven or oven set at 200-220°C/400-425°F for about 10-15 minutes, turning over halfway through the cooking time. Times will depend upon the thickness of the bread and its composition.

TOAST: Toast can be made using a special hinged toaster available with some range-style cookers. This is rather like the hinged wire flip grills that are used for cooking on barbecues making it easy to turn foods in one simple operation and these will also work well on the range-style cooker. Place the bread between the hinged wires and cook on top of the Boiling Plate until golden, turn over and cook the remaining side. This method is of course unsuitable for a range-style cooker with gas hob rather than hotplate top.

BACON AND BRIE FEUILLETE

SERVES 6

15 g (½ oz) butter or margarine

100 g (4 oz) smoked back bacon, rinds removed and chopped

3 onions, chopped

50 g (2 oz) Cheddar cheese, grated

1 tablespoon snipped chives

1 teaspoon seeded mustard

freshly ground black pepper

400 g (14 oz) frozen puff pastry, thawed

175 g (6 oz) Brie, finely sliced

beaten egg, to glaze

 This is a wonderful golden puff pastry envelope filled with smoked bacon, onion and Brie perfect for an outdoor brunch, lunch or picnic. The feuillete can be served warm from the oven or refrigerated and served cold with a selection of crisp seasonal salads.

Melt the butter or margarine in a large heavy-based pan, add the bacon and onion and cook until lightly browned and softened, about 8 minutes. Remove with a slotted spoon and allow to cool.

Mix the Cheddar cheese with the chives, mustard and pepper to taste.

Cut the pastry in half and roll out each piece, on a lightly floured surface, to a rectangle measuring 25 x 30 cm (10 x 12 inches). Place one piece on a wetted baking sheet. Spoon the onion mixture over the top to within 2.5 cm (1 inch) of the edges. Top with the cheese mixture, spreading evenly and then with the sliced Brie. Brush the pastry edges with beaten egg then cover with the second piece of pastry to make a lid. Press the edges firmly to seal, trim and flute attractively. Use any pastry trimmings to decorate the top of the feuillete. Glaze with beaten egg.

2 **4** 2 OVEN RANGE AND 4 OVEN RANGE: Cook in the Roasting Oven with the grid shelf on the third set of runners for 15 minutes. Lower the grid shelf to the bottom set of runners and cook for a further 15 minutes, covering with foil if necessary, until golden and cooked.

THERMODIAL-CONTROLLED RANGE: Cook in the top of the oven set 220°C/425°F for 30 minutes, covering with foil if necessary, until golden and cooked through.

Serve warm or cold with a selection of seasonal salads.

HAM AND EGG BRUNCH NESTS

MAKES 8

2 slices white bread,
crusts removed

---

15 g (½ oz) butter

---

2 tablespoons olive oil

---

1 garlic clove, crushed

---

1 teaspoon snipped chives

---

4 large 'beef' tomatoes or
2 large peppers

---

8 slices thin-cut, dry-cured,
smoked ham

---

salt and pepper

---

8 eggs

8-12 tiny button mushrooms

---

butter to dot

Here is the all-British favourite, ham and eggs, with a continental twist because they are baked in a half shell or nest of 'beef' tomato and topped with herb and garlic croûtons. I like to use these hand-sized tomatoes since they have a sweeter taste but you could just as easily use large ordinary tomatoes or even half shells of sweet red, orange or green peppers (but blanch in boiling water for 5 minutes before filling). These make a splendid brunch dish for late Sunday morning entertaining.

Cut the bread slices into small cubes. Melt the butter with the olive oil in a large heavy-based pan. When hot and sizzling add the garlic and cook for ½ minute. Add the bread cubes and cook until golden on all sides.

Remove from the pan with a slotted spoon and allow to drain on absorbent kitchen paper. While still hot toss in the chives and keep warm on the hotplate.

Remove the tops from the tomatoes, scoop out the flesh and drain well upside down on absorbent kitchen paper. Alternatively, halve the peppers across their middles then scoop out the flesh and seeds.

Place the tomatoes or peppers in a greased baking dish. Carefully tuck a slice of ham into each tomato or pepper half then crack in an egg. Season with salt and pepper to taste and dot with a little butter.

2 4 2 OVEN RANGE AND 4 OVEN RANGE: Place the dish on the grid shelf set on the lowest set of runners in the Roasting Oven for about 15-20 minutes or until the eggs are just set. Serve hot scattered with the garlic and herb croutons.

 THERMODIAL-CONTROLLED RANGE: Cook in the oven set at 190°C/ 375°F for 15-20 minutes or until the eggs are just set.

Serve straight from the dish with warm crusty bread.

SUNDAY BRUNCH CLUB SANDWICHES

SERVES 2

6 rashers bacon, rinds removed

6 slices freshly-made toast

about 4 tablespoons mayonnaise

lettuce leaves

2 large slices cooked turkey

salt and pepper

1 large tomato, sliced

 Who invented and christened the club sandwich? And how, where and when? No authoritative answers to these questions are available. One legend has it that a man came home late and hungry from his club one night, raided the refrigerator and made himself a super sandwich which he dubbed 'club'. Another says that the chef of a club made himself a reputation by devising this special sandwich. Whatever the answer, club sandwiches are intended to serve as more or less adequate substitutes for a full meal, offering bread, meat and salad, and may consist of anything from three to about five stories. The foundation is always toast, but the superstructure can be almost anything you like. This is the perfect one to serve for Sunday Brunch.

Place the bacon in a lightly greased roasting tin.

2 4 2 OVEN RANGE AND 4 OVEN RANGE: Cook on the floor of the Roasting Oven until crisp and golden, about 6-8 minutes, turning over once halfway through cooking.

THERMODIAL-CONTROLLED RANGE: Cook on the floor of the oven set at 200-220°C/400-425°F until crisp and golden, about 6-8 minutes, turning over once halfway through cooking.

Drain on absorbent kitchen paper.

Spread one side of each slice of toast with mayonnaise. Arrange lettuce leaves on two slices of toast, top each with a slice of turkey. Season to taste then add another slice of toast, mayonnaise side up.

Add more lettuce, half the tomato slices and three rashers of cooked bacon to each sandwich. Top with the remaining toast slices, mayonnaise side down. Cut the sandwiches into quarters and secure each one with a cocktail stick. Arrange, cut sides up, on individual plates to serve.

BREAKFAST SCONES

MAKES 12-14

450 g (1 lb) floury potatoes
(King Edward's or Maris Piper
for example)

salt and pepper

350 g (12 oz) self-raising flour

2 teaspoons baking powder

75 g (3 oz) butter or margarine

75 g (3 oz) smoked cooked
ham, chopped

50 g (2 oz) smoked cooked
sausage, chopped

2½ tablespoons snipped chives

4 tablespoons milk

4-5 tablespoons natural yogurt

milk, to brush

 Potato scones flavoured with smoked ham and sausage make a welcome change to bread at breakfast or brunch time. Serve warm straight from the oven, split and buttered. This would also be a good way to use the potato scooped out when making crispy potato skins (see page 27).

Peel and cut the potatoes into chunks. Place in a pan with just enough salted water to cover, bring to the boil and cook until tender, about 12-15 minutes. Drain thoroughly then sieve or purée in a processor until smooth.

Sift the flour with the baking powder into a bowl. Rub in the butter or margarine until the mixture resembles fine breadcrumbs. Stir in the ham, sausage and chives with the cooked potato, milk and sufficient yogurt to mix to a firm but pliable dough. Knead lightly then roll out, on a lightly floured surface, to about 2 cm (¾ inch) thick. Stamp out about 12-14 scones using a 6 cm (2½ inch) biscuit cutter, re-rolling where necessary.

Place on a lightly greased baking sheet and brush with milk to glaze.

 2 OVEN RANGE: Cook in the Roasting Oven with the grid shelf on the lowest set of runners and the cold plain shelf above for about 25 minutes or until golden.

 4 OVEN RANGE: Cook in the Baking Oven with the grid shelf on the second set of runners for about 25-30 minutes or until golden.

THERMODIAL-CONTROLLED RANGE: Cook in the oven set at 180°C/350°F for 25-30 minutes or until golden.

Allow to cool on a wire rack.

VERY SPECIAL OMELETTE

SERVES 2

5 large eggs (size 1 or 2)

2 tablespoons aquavit

salt and pepper

25 g (1 oz) unsalted butter

100 g (4 oz) smoked salmon, thinly sliced

2 spring onions, finely chopped

150 ml (¼ pint) soured cream

black pumpernickel bread, to serve

An omelette recipe all the better for serving on a special occasion like a birthday or anniversary breakfast with Champagne or for sharing with special friends on a lazy, self-indulgent Sunday for brunch.

Whisk the eggs with the aquavit and salt and pepper to taste.

2 4 🌡 2 OVEN RANGE, 4 OVEN RANGE, THERMODIAL-CONTROLLED RANGE: Heat a large omelette pan on the Boiling Plate until hot, add the butter and heat until melted and the foam subsides. Add the egg mixture, transfer immediately to the Simmering Plate and cook until the omelette is just set but still soft and moist. Arrange the smoked salmon over the omelette, sprinkle with the spring onions and spoon over 3 heaped tablespoons of the soured cream. Cook for a further 10-15 seconds or until the underside is golden, fold over into half then slide onto a heated serving plate.

Cut the omelette into half to serve with the remaining soured cream and pumpernickel bread.

VARIATION

Smoked Salmon and Caviar Omelette: If you like, the spring onions can be replaced with caviar or mock caviar. You will need about 3 tablespoons for the filling and an extra tablespoon to serve with the soured cream.

CRANACHAN WITH ALPINE STRAWBERRIES

SERVES 4

225 ml (8 fl oz) thick Greek yogurt, strained

225 g (8 oz) fromage blanc

75 ml (3 fl oz) whisky

4-5 tablespoons clear honey

75 g (3 oz) medium oatmeal

350 g (12 oz) alpine strawberries or other berries, hulled

mint sprigs, to decorate

Follow the example of the canny Scots and mix tiny but flavoursome alpine strawberries or wild strawberries with fromage blanc, yogurt, whisky, honey and oven-toasted oatmeal to make a special sweet dessert-style dish perfect to round off a brunch – the result is more mouth-watering and attractive than porridge! Any other decorative berry could be used instead like raspberries, loganberries and sweet plump blackberries.

Mix the yogurt with the fromage blanc, whisky and honey, blending well. Place the oatmeal on a baking sheet and spread out evenly.

2 4 2 OVEN RANGE AND 4 OVEN RANGE: Cook on the floor of the Roasting Oven for about 15-20 minutes or until golden, stirring occasionally so that it browns evenly.

THERMODIAL-CONTROLLED RANGE: Cook in the oven set at 180°C/ 350°F for about 20 minutes or until golden, stirring occasionally so that it browns evenly.

Allow to cool then stir into the yogurt mixture, cover and chill thoroughly.

To serve, layer the oatmeal mixture with the berries in stemmed dessert glasses, finishing with a few berries. Decorate with mint sprigs and leave to stand for 30 minutes before serving.

GINGER AND ALMOND MUFFINS

MAKES 8

100 g (4 oz) plain flour

1½ teaspoons baking powder

½ teaspoon salt

25 g (1 oz) ground almonds

40 g (1½ oz) caster sugar

150 ml (¼ pint) milk

1½ teaspoons ginger wine

1 tablespoon lemon juice

25 ml (1 fl oz) sunflower oil

1 small egg (size 4 or 5)

175 g (6 oz) crystallised or very well-drained stem ginger, coarsely chopped

crushed sugar cubes (optional)

Ever since I worked in New York in my early twenties I've had a passion for American-style muffins whether for breakfast, elevenses, tea or as a snack. My daughter Lucinda has caught the bug and now comes up with ideas for good flavour combinations. This recipe provides a fairly sophisticated flavour – perfect for serving to adults at breakfast or brunch with soft cheese and honey or home-made preserves. Muffin pans or patty pans and large muffin-style paper cases are now on sale in many cookware shops throughout the country. The muffins are best eaten on the day of making but can also be frozen successfully then quickly refreshed in the oven before serving.

Sift the flour with the baking powder and salt into a bowl. Add the almonds and sugar and mix well. Beat the milk with the ginger wine, lemon juice, oil and egg. Add to the dry ingredients with the chopped ginger and mix to make a fairly lumpy looking mixture. Do not overmix the ingredients or they will not be light and fluffy when cooked.

Spoon evenly into 8 paper muffin cases set in a muffin or patty tin. Sprinkle with crushed sugar cubes to decorate if you prefer.

2 OVEN RANGE: Bake in the Roasting Oven with the grid shelf on the lowest set of runners or oven floor for about 20-25 minutes, turning the tin once for even browning, until well-risen and golden.

4 OVEN RANGE: Bake in the top of the Baking Oven for about 20-25 minutes, turning the tin once for even browning, until well-risen and golden.

THERMODIAL-CONTROLLED RANGE: Bake in the oven set at 190°C/ 375°F for 25 minutes turning the tin once for even browning, until well-risen and golden.

Allow to cool in the tin for 5 minutes then transfer to a wire rack to cool completely. Store in an airtight tin until required but best eaten on day of making.

BACON AND SWEETCORN QUICHE

SERVES 4-6

175 g (6 oz) wholemeal
shortcrust pastry

Filling

100 g (4 oz) bacon, chopped

1 onion, finely chopped

175 g (6 oz) sweetcorn kernels

3 small eggs, beaten

150 g (5 oz) natural yogurt

1 teaspoon made mustard

100 g (4 oz) Cheddar cheese,
grated

salt and pepper

2 tomatoes, skinned and sliced

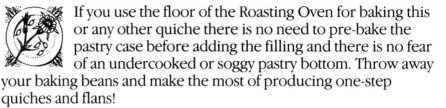

If you use the floor of the Roasting Oven for baking this or any other quiche there is no need to pre-bake the pastry case before adding the filling and there is no fear of an undercooked or soggy pastry bottom. Throw away your baking beans and make the most of producing one-step quiches and flans!

Roll out the pastry on a lightly-floured surface and use to line a 20 cm (8 inch) loose-bottomed flan tin. Chill while preparing the filling.

Cook the bacon gently in a pan on the Simmering Plate until the fat runs then transfer to the Boiling Plate and fry until crisp. Remove with a slotted spoon and reserve. Add the onion to the bacon juices and cover and cook until just tender, about 4-5 minutes. Add the sweetcorn and continue cooking for 2 minutes.

Mix the eggs with the yogurt, mustard, 75 g (3 oz) of the cheese and salt and pepper to taste. Add the bacon, sweetcorn and onion mixture and mix well. Spoon into the prepared flan case. Sprinkle with the remaining cheese and arrange the tomato slices around the edge.

2 4 2 OVEN RANGE AND 4 OVEN RANGE: Place the tin on the floor of the oven and cook for about 30 minutes until the top is golden and set, turning the tin once during cooking for even browning.

THERMODIAL-CONTROLLED RANGE: Place the tin on the floor of the oven set at 190°C/375°F for about 30 minutes or until the top is golden and set, turning the tin once during cooking for even browning.

Serve warm or cold cut into wedges with salad.

FISH AND SEAFOOD

BAKING FISH

Prepare the fish according to variety and leave plain or stuff or cut into fillets for cooking. Place in a greased baking dish and season with salt and pepper to taste and drizzle with a little lemon juice. Dot with a little butter or margarine if you like but this is not strictly necessary. Cover with foil or greaseproof paper. Timings will depend very much upon the size of the fish, the thickness and the density of the flesh but the following times are good guidelines:

 2 OVEN RANGE AND 4 OVEN RANGE: Cook in the Roasting Oven with the grid shelf on the second set of runners.

THERMODIAL-CONTROLLED RANGE: Cook in the top half of the oven set at 190°C (375°F).

TYPE	COOKING TIME
Thin fish fillets	12-15 minutes
Rolled or folded fish fillets	15-20 minutes
Fish steaks	25-30 minutes
Whole flat fish	25-30 minutes
Thick whole fish	30-35 minutes

POACHING FISH

Whether you choose to poach a king-sized salmon or a few smoked haddock fillets for a breakfast kedgeree, the results will be perfect. Choose from three methods – one using a fish kettle on the hob, the second using the hob and oven and the third using the oven only.

FISH KETTLE METHOD

This is suitable for large whole fish like salmon and salmon trout. Clean and scale the fish and stuff the inner cavity with a few slices of lemon. Lay in the fish kettle and add just enough good fish stock or court bouillon to cover.

2 **4** 🌡 2 OVEN RANGE, 4 OVEN RANGE AND THERMODIAL-CONTROLLED RANGE: Bring slowly to the boil then simmer for the recommended time:

WEIGHT	COOKING TIME
up to 2.25 kg (5 lb)	5 minutes
2.25 kg (5 lb) to 3.15 kg (7 lb)	7-9 minutes
3.25 kg (7 lb) to 4.5 kg (10 lb)	10-12 minutes

HOB AND OVEN POACHED METHOD

This is suitable for small whole fish like trout and sole and for fish fillets like haddock, plaice and cod. Place the fish in a shallow pan with about 600 ml (1 pint) of good fish stock or court bouillon. Bring to the boil on the Boiling Plate, transfer to the Simmering Plate for 2 minutes.

2 **4** 2 OVEN RANGE AND 4 OVEN RANGE: Transfer to the Simmering Oven and cook for 10 minutes per 450 g (1 lb) plus 10 minutes.

 THERMODIAL-CONTROLLED RANGE: Transfer to the oven set at 150-160°C/300-325°F and cook for 10 minutes per 450 g (1 lb) plus 10 minutes.

OVEN POACHED METHOD

This is suitable for cooking large whole fish when a fish kettle is not available. Clean and scale the fish, removing the head and wrap in buttered foil. Place in a large roasting tin and half cover with boiling water or court bouillon.

2 **4** 2 OVEN RANGE AND 4 OVEN RANGE: Cook in the Roasting Oven on the bottom set of runners for 10 minutes per 450 g (1 lb), turning the fish halfway through the calculated cooking time. Allow to cool in the foil until warm enough to handle.

THERMODIAL-CONTROLLED RANGE: Cook in the oven set at 190-200°C/375-400°F for 10 minutes per 450 g (1 lb), turning the fish halfway through the calculated cooking time. Allow to cool in the foil until warm enough to handle.

GRILLING FISH

It is possible to 'grill' in the top part of the Roasting Oven or in the top of a very hot oven using a baking tray or on a grill rack in a roasting tin. It is also possible to use the hotplate with a cast-iron ridged grill pan.

GRILLING IN THE OVEN

Brush the fish with oil and place on a baking tray or on the grill rack in a roasting tin.

2 **4** 2 OVEN RANGE AND 4 OVEN RANGE: Cook in the Roasting Oven with the grid shelf on the highest set of runners, turning the fish over halfway through cooking. Times depend very much upon the thickness of the fish – thin fillets may take as little as 2 minutes each side and larger steaks up to 5 minutes each side.

THERMODIAL-CONTROLLED RANGE: Cook in the top of the oven set at 230-240°C/450-475°F, turning the fish over halfway through cooking. Times depend very much upon the thickness of the fish – thin fillets may take as little as 2 minutes each side and larger steaks up to 5 minutes each side.

GRILLING USING A CAST-IRON RIDGED GRILL PAN

Brush the fish with oil on both sides and dip in a little seasoned flour.

2 **4** 2 OVEN RANGE, 4 OVEN RANGE AND THERMODIAL-CONTROLLED RANGE: Place the grill pan on the Boiling Plate or the hottest part of the hotplate and heat for a few minutes. Add the fish and press down lightly. Move onto the Simmering Plate or along to the cooler end of the hotplate and cook depending upon thickness, turning over once. Thin fillets may need only 2 minutes per side and thicker steaks or whole fish may need 5-10 minutes each side.

STEAMING FISH

Fish can be steamed on the hob or in the oven as steaks, fillets or whole fish.

STEAMING ON THE HOB

Place the prepared fish on cooking foil and sprinkle with salt and pepper to taste. Wrap up to enclose and place in the steamer, fish kettle or between two greased plates on top of a pan. Steam over gently boiling water for the recommended time:

TYPE	COOKING TIME
Fish fillets	15-20 minutes
Fish steaks, middle cuts and whole fish	30 minutes per 450 g
	(1 lb) plus 5 minutes

STEAMING IN THE OVEN

This is suitable for whole fish, middle cuts of fish and fish fillets. Place the prepared fish in a buttered baking dish, season to taste then add a little water, milk or fish stock to moisten. Cover with a lid or foil.

2 **4** 2 OVEN RANGE AND 4 OVEN RANGE: Cook in the Roasting Oven for 5 minutes then transfer to the Simmering Oven for about 20 minutes until the fish is cooked and will flake easily. Remove the fish from the juices with a slotted spoon to serve.

THERMODIAL-CONTROLLED RANGE: Cook in the oven set at 180°C/ 350°F for about 15-20 minutes depending upon the thickness of the fish until cooked through and the flesh will flake easily. Remove the fish from the juices with a slotted spoon to serve.

FRYING FISH

Fish can be fried on the hob in the normal way but can also be fried on the floor of the oven with good results. I particularly like to cook fish this way since cooking smells are reduced to a minimum. Coat the fish in seasoned flour, a light batter, breadcrumbs or oatmeal as liked. Pour just enough oil into a heavy-based roasting tin to cover the base.

2 **4** 2 OVEN RANGE AND 4 OVEN RANGE: Place the tin on the floor of the Roasting Oven and heat until a blue haze appears. Add the fish and cook according to size and thickness, turning over once during the cooking time. Drain on absorbent kitchen paper.

THERMODIAL-CONTROLLED RANGE: Place the tin on the floor of the oven set at 220-230°C/425-450°F and heat until a blue haze appears. Add the fish and cook according to size and thickness, turning over once during the cooking time. Drain on absorbent kitchen paper.

SALMON KOULIBIACA WITH CUCUMBER SAUCE

SERVES 8

50 g (2 oz) butter or margarine

1 small leek, finely shredded

175 g (6 oz) assorted mushrooms

1½ tablespoons lemon juice

1 teaspoon chopped fresh dill

1 tablespoon chopped fresh parsley

salt and pepper

350 g (12 oz) puff pastry

100 g (4 oz) cooked brown rice

350 g (12 oz) cooked salmon

2 hard-boiled eggs, shelled and coarsely chopped

4 tablespoons soured cream

beaten egg, to glaze

fresh dill, to garnish

Sauce

½ cucumber, finely chopped

150 ml (¼ pint) mayonnaise

150 ml (¼ pint) natural thick yogurt

grated rind of ½ lemon

1 teaspoon chopped fresh dill

A wonderful dish that can be prepared well ahead of cooking. Russian inspired, the salmon in this dish is eked out with rice, hard-boiled eggs and mushrooms. I like to use brown rice, and an assortment of mushrooms for added interest but white rice and plain button mushrooms will suffice. A quickly-made cucumber sauce provides the finishing touch.

Melt the butter or margarine in a pan, add the leek and cook until softened, about 4-5 minutes. Add the mushrooms, cut into bite-sized pieces, and lemon juice and cook until just tender, about 2-3 minutes. Remove from the heat and add the dill, parsley and salt and pepper to taste. Skin and bone the salmon and cut into bite-size pieces.

Divide the pastry in half and roll out each piece, on a lightly floured surface, then cut to a rectangle measuring 30 x 18 cm (12 x 7 inches), reserving any pastry trimmings. Place one piece on a greased baking sheet and top with half of the cooked rice. Spread over the pastry to within 2.5 cm (1 inch) of the edges. Cover with half of the mushroom mixture, then the pieces of fish and the chopped eggs. Top with the remaining mushroom mixture and finally the remaining rice. Dot the soured cream over the entire mixture.

Brush the pastry edges with beaten egg then top with the second pastry piece. Pinch the edges of the pastry together to seal and crimp attractively. Glaze the pastry with beaten egg, decorate with any pastry trimmings and glaze again.

2 **4** 2 OVEN RANGE AND 4 OVEN RANGE: Cook in the Roasting Oven with the grid shelf on the third set of runners, for about 30 minutes, or until the pastry is well-risen, crisp and golden.

THERMODIAL-CONTROLLED RANGE: Cook in the oven set at 220°C/425°F for about 30 minutes, or until the pastry is well-risen, crisp and golden.

Meanwhile, to prepare the sauce, mix the cucumber with the mayonnaise, yogurt, lemon, dill and salt and pepper to taste. Chill until required.

Serve the koulibiaca hot cut into thick slices with the chilled cucumber sauce. Garnish with sprigs of fresh feathery dill.

MONKFISH WITH BURNT ORANGE SAUCE

 The firm white flesh of monkfish responds well to oven cooking and the delicate taste is enhanced by the tangy flavour of this orange-based sauce. When monkfish is unavailable any other firm white fish may be used like turbot, brill or John Dory.

SERVES 4

4 x 250 g (9 oz) monkfish tails, skinned

salt and pepper

60 g (2½ oz) butter

2 tablespoons olive oil

grated zest of 1 orange

juice of 2 oranges

1½ tablespoons caster sugar

1½ tablespoons water

½ clove garlic, crushed

1 shallot, finely chopped

½ stick celery, shredded into fine julienne

1½ teaspoons flour

½-1 teaspoon sherry vinegar

Dry the monkfish tails with absorbent kitchen paper then season with salt and pepper to taste. Place 15 g (½ oz) of the butter and the oil in a roasting tin and heat until hot. Add the monkfish tails and cook quickly to sear on all sides, about 2 minutes. Add one quarter of the orange juice and half of the grated orange zest. Remove from the heat, cover the pan with buttered paper.

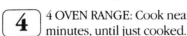

2 **2 OVEN RANGE:** Cook on the grid shelf set on the lowest set of runners with the cold plain shelf above for about 10-12 minutes, until just cooked.

4 **4 OVEN RANGE:** Cook near the top of the Baking Oven for about 10-12 minutes, until just cooked.

 THERMODIAL-CONTROLLED RANGE: Cook in the oven set at 180°C/350°F for about 10-12 minutes, until just cooked.

Remove from the oven and leave to stand on the Warming Plate or on top of the Simmering Hob lid to complete cooking and keep warm.

Meanwhile, place the sugar in a heavy-based pan, add the water and stir over a gentle heat until dissolved. Increase the heat and cook until the sugar caramelises to a rich, golden brown. Remove from the heat and add the remaining orange juice (take care there may be some spluttering). Stir over a gentle heat to blend well.

Melt the remaining butter in a small pan, add the garlic, shallot and celery and cook until softened, about 3 minutes. Add the flour and cook for 1 minute until the mixture turns a golden colour. Add the prepared caramel mixture a little at a time, mixing well to keep the sauce smooth. Bring to the boil and cook until thickened. Add the remaining orange zest and mix well.

Strain the juices from the fish and add to the burnt orange sauce, mixing well. Fillet the monkfish tails and slice into medallions. Arrange on four heated serving plates. Add sherry vinegar to taste to the sauce then spoon over and around the monkfish medallions. Serve at once.

OPPOSITE:
Ham and Egg Brunch
Nests

GRILLED RED MULLET WITH ORANGE SALSA

SERVES 4

2 oranges

1 tablespoon red wine vinegar

4 tablespoons olive oil

a few drops of chilli sauce or
1-2 teaspoons chilli seasoning

salt

4 red mullet, scaled and
cleaned
or 4 large redfish fillets

2 large, firm tomatoes, peeled
and diced

4 spring onions, trimmed

1 red chilli, seeded and
chopped (optional)

fresh coriander sprigs, to
garnish

Whole fish chargrill really well and quickly on a range-style cooker using a cast-iron grill pan with a ridged base – the result is so near to barbecuing that I defy you to tell the difference. Redfish look and taste especially good, but you could use other fish like mackerel, sardines, bream, or cutlets of whole fish such as swordfish or tuna.

Finely grate the zest and squeeze the juice from one of the oranges into a small bowl. Add the wine vinegar, oil, chilli sauce and salt to taste and beat well to blend. Place the prepared fish into a shallow dish and pour over the prepared marinade. Cover and leave to stand for 10-15 minutes whilst preparing the remaining ingredients.

2 **4** 🌡️ 2 OVEN RANGE, 4 OVEN RANGE, THERMODIAL-CONTROLLED RANGE: Remove about half of the peel from the remaining orange, and cut into fine julienne strips. Place in a pan of water and simmer for 5-10 minutes, then drain and set aside.

Remove and discard the remaining peel and pith from the orange then chop the flesh into small pieces. Add the chopped tomato, 2 chopped spring onions, the chilli if used and salt to taste. Chill until required.

Heat the ridged cast-iron grill pan on the Boiling Plate until hot, about 3-4 minutes. Add the fish (you may have to cook them two at a time if large) and press down to ensure full contact with the base. Cook for about 2-4 minutes each side, depending upon size and thickness, basting with the marinade juices several times. Cover the pan with a lid if possible to prevent spluttering. When cooked, transfer to a heated serving dish and top with the orange julienne, remaining spring onions cut into diagonal strips and garnish with fresh coriander.

Serve at once with the well-chilled orange salsa. Baked jacket potatoes and a green bean salad make excellent accompaniments.

OPPOSITE:
Grilled Red Mullet with
Orange Salsa

BEST-EVER SEAFOOD PAELLA

SERVES 6-8

about ½ teaspoon saffron strands

600 ml (1 pint) fish stock

2 tablespoons olive oil

1 large onion, chopped

3 cloves garlic, crushed

225 g (8 oz) tomatoes, peeled, seeded and chopped

100 g (4 oz) squid, cleaned and sliced

about 12 mussels in their shells, scrubbed

225 g (8 oz) Spanish paella rice or long-grain white rice

salt and pepper

450 g (1 lb) cooked seafood (prawns, mussels, shrimps and scallops for example)

1 large red pepper, cored, seeded and finely sliced

100 g (4 oz) frozen peas

1 x 60 g (2½ oz) can dressed crab

3 tablespoons chopped fresh parsley

whole prawns in their shells, to garnish

I call this best-ever because I've sampled many paellas and this one has to be the most tasty. I think the secret ingredient is the can of dressed crab which is added to the mixture at the end of cooking but of course you will also need the very freshest selection of assorted seafood like squid, scallops, prawns and mussels for success. Saffron will also give the best flavour but if you find it hard to buy use ½ teaspoon turmeric instead.

Place the saffron strands in a small bowl. Heat 150 ml (¼ pint) of the fish stock until boiling then pour over the saffron strands. Cover and leave to soak.

Heat the oil in a large pan on the Simmering Plate. Add the onion and garlic and cook for 5 minutes. Transfer to the Boiling Plate and add the tomatoes, squid and mussels in their shells. Cook for 2 minutes or until the mussels are cooked and the shells are open. Remove with a slotted spoon and reserve.

Add the rice to the tomato mixture with the remaining stock, mixing well. Strain the stock from the saffron strands and add to the rice mixture with salt and pepper to taste. Bring to the boil and cover.

2 OVEN RANGE AND 4 OVEN RANGE: Transfer to the floor of the Simmering Oven and cook for 25 minutes. Remove from the oven and add the cooked seafood, red pepper and peas, mixing well. Re-cover, return to the oven and cook for a further 5-10 minutes or until the rice is tender and all of the liquid has been absorbed.

THERMODIAL-CONTROLLED RANGE: Transfer to the oven set at 160°C/ 325°F and cook for 25 minutes. Remove from the oven and add the cooked seafood, red pepper and peas, mixing well. Re-cover, return to the oven and cook for a further 5-10 minutes or until the rice is tender and all of the liquid has been absorbed.

Return to the Simmering Plate and add the dressed crab and parsley, mixing well. Stir for 1 minute to heat through then spoon into a heated serving dish. Serve garnished with whole prawns in their shell and the cooked mussels in their shells.

BADANLOCH CREAM SALMON

SERVES 4

2 tail pieces salmon, filleted to give 4 x 100-150 g (4-5 oz) fillets

25-50 g (1-2 oz) butter or margarine

salt and pepper

about 4 sprigs fresh mint

½ lemon, halved

150 ml (¼ pint) medium white wine

½ cucumber, peeled

150 ml (¼ pint) double cream or crème fraîche

mint or parsley sprigs, to garnish

 This is a very delicately mint-flavoured salmon in sauce dish. The fish pieces are wrapped in greased greaseproof paper for poaching so they are easier to remove from the pan and handle when just cooked. Serve with new potatoes in their skins and a crisp green vegetable or seasonal salad.

2 | 4 | 🌡 2 OVEN RANGE, 4 OVEN RANGE, THERMODIAL-CONTROLLED RANGE: Top each piece of fish with a few knobs of butter or margarine, salt and pepper to taste and a few mint leaves. Wrap individually in greased greaseproof paper with the join underneath.

Half-fill a frying pan with 150 ml (¼ pint) water, squeeze in the juice from the lemon then add the squeezed pieces and the wine. Bring to simmering point on the Boiling Plate and carefully add the parcels.

Transfer immediately to the Simmering Plate and let the mixture bubble for 2-3 minutes, basting occasionally.

Meanwhile thickly slice the cucumber then cut the slices in half. Remove the fish parcels from the stock, unwrap and pour any cooking juices back into the pan. Keep the fish warm. Add the remaining mint and simmer the mixture until reduced by half.

Add the cucumber pieces and gently poach until the cucumber is just tender but still crunchy, about 4 minutes. Remove the cucumber with a slotted spoon and keep warm. Simmer the juices until reduced again to about one half. Add the cream and simmer very gently until slightly thickened. Remove and discard the mint sprigs and check and adjust the seasoning if necessary.

Place the salmon fillets on individual warmed serving plates with the cooked cucumber. Spoon over the mint-flavoured sauce and garnish with a mint or parsley sprig to serve.

SPECIAL FRIDAY FISH PIE

SERVES 4-6

675 g (1½ lb) boneless smoked haddock fillet

450 ml (¾ pint) milk

900 g (2 lb) potatoes, peeled and diced

75 g (3 oz) butter or margarine

salt and pepper

450 g (1 lb) spinach, trimmed and cooked until tender

6 eggs or 12 quail's eggs

100 g (4 oz) peeled prawns

150 ml (¼ pint) double cream

1 tablespoon chopped fresh tarragon

pinch of ground nutmeg

 Here is a fish pie good enough to serve to friends for supper and special enough for a dinner party if tiny quail's eggs are used instead of hen's eggs. If piping is your forte then pipe the creamed potato over the fish filling for special effect.

2 **4** 2 OVEN RANGE AND 4 OVEN RANGE: Place the fish in a baking dish with the milk and cook in the Roasting Oven for about 12-15 minutes or until the fish is cooked and will flake easily. Remove the fish from the milk and allow to cool.

Cook the potatoes in boiling salted water on the Boiling Plate until tender, about 20 minutes. Drain, add a little of the fish cooking milk and half of the butter and mash until smooth and creamy. Season generously with salt and pepper to taste.

Spread the remaining butter over the base and sides of a shallow 1.5 litre (3 pint) ovenproof dish. Spread the spinach over the base. Make 6 or 12 small hollows in the spinach and crack a raw egg into each. Flake the fish into bite-sized pieces and scatter over the top with the prawns. Mix the cream with the tarragon and nutmeg and spoon over the fish. Spread or pipe the potato over the fish to cover completely.

Cook in the Roasting Oven with the grid shelf on the second set of runners for about 30 minutes or until cooked and golden.

THERMODIAL-CONTROLLED RANGE: Prepare as above but cook the fish in the oven set at 190°C/375°F for about 12-15 minutes until cooked. Cook the potatoes on the Boiling Plate until tender, about 20 minutes. Cook the pie in the oven set at 190°C/375°F for about 25-30 minutes until cooked and golden.

BILOXI FISH STEW

Mississippi belongs very much to the traditional Deep South and its cuisine combines that of the high living plantation house, together with the much poorer style of residence. Biloxi fish stew straddles both easily since the fish chosen reflects the high or low standard of living. One of Mississippi's favourite fish, the tasty but rather ugly Catfish, is often used for this recipe which is wonderfully warming on a cold day.

2 **4** 🌡️ 2 OVEN RANGE, 4 OVEN RANGE, THERMODIAL-CONTROLLED RANGE: Melt the butter or margarine in a large heavy-based pan. Add the onion, celery and green pepper and sauté until tender, about 5-8 minutes. Sprinkle with the flour and chilli powder and mix well. Gradually add the stock, bring to the boil, stirring constantly. Transfer to the Simmering Plate, cover and simmer for 15 minutes.

Add the tomatoes, peas, vinegar, sugar and fish, mixing well and simmer for 10 minutes.

Add the prawns, sherry, Tabasco sauce and salt to taste and heat through gently.

Serve hot with cooked American-style long-grain rice.

SERVES 4-6

50 g (2 oz) butter or margarine

1 large onion, sliced

2 sticks celery, sliced

1 green pepper, cored, seeded and sliced

1 tablespoon plain flour

2 teaspoons chilli powder

300 ml (½ pint) light or fish stock

1 x 425 g (15 oz) can chopped tomatoes

225 g (8 oz) frozen peas

1 tablespoon cider vinegar

1 tablespoon brown sugar

450 g (1 lb) white fish, skinned and cubed (cod, monkfish or haddock for example)

225 g (8 oz) cooked peeled prawns

150 ml (¼ pint) dry sherry

Tabasco sauce

salt

PINK TROUT IN CHAMPAGNE SAUCE WITH WILD RICE

SERVES 6

6 x 350 g (12 oz) pink trout, gutted and heads removed

3 tablespoons lemon juice

salt

40 g (1½ oz) butter, softened

250 ml (8 fl oz) dry Champagne

6 tablespoons dry vermouth

250 ml (8 fl oz) fish stock

25 g (1 oz) plain flour

150 ml (¼ pint) double cream, chilled

sprigs of fresh dill, to garnish

cooked wild rice, to serve

Chilled pink trout and Champagne herald the height of the summer to me with memories of happy garden lunch parties or balmy summer evening conservatory suppers. Here is my smart alternative, certainly special enough for a formal summer dinner, poached pink trout served in a creamy Champagne, vermouth and lemon sauce. Serve equally stylishly garnished with feathery dill and cooked wild rice.

2 **4** 🌡 2 OVEN RANGE, 4 OVEN RANGE, THERMODIAL-CONTROLLED RANGE: Sprinkle the trout with the lemon juice and salt to taste. Spread half of the butter over a large poaching tin or fish kettle, add the Champagne, dry vermouth and stock and bring to the boil. Add the fish, cover and cook over a very gentle heat until just cooked, about 3-5 minutes. Remove from the liquid with a slotted spoon and carefully remove the skins. Keep warm.

Boil the poaching liquid until it is reduced to about 300 ml (½ pint). Meanwhile, mix the remaining butter with the flour to make a paste. Carefully whisk small pieces of this paste into the liquid a little at a time. Bring to the boil and simmer for 2 minutes or until the sauce is smooth and thickened. Season with salt and pepper to taste. Remove from the heat, cover and keep warm.

Whip the chilled cream until it stands in soft peaks. Stir one quarter of the cream into the sauce, mixing well then fold in the remaining cream gently but thoroughly.

Arrange the cooked pink trout on heated serving plates and spoon over the sauce. Serve at once, garnished with feathery sprigs of dill and accompanied with cooked wild rice.

LANDLUBBERS TUNA WITH GREEN PEPPERCORN SAUCE

SERVES 4

1 x 100 g (3½ oz) jar green peppercorns in brine

60 g (2½ oz) honey

1½ tablespoons olive oil

freshly ground black pepper

4 tuna steaks, cut about 2 cm (¾ inch) thick and weighing about 225 g (8 oz) each

100 g (4 oz) unsalted butter

2-3 tablespoons vegetable oil

A few years ago I would have hesitated in including this recipe in anything but a specialist cookery book since tuna was so hard to find. Now it seems that every fishmonger and quality supermarket stocks fresh tuna in either fillets or steaks. Here it is marinated in a green peppercorn, honey and olive mixture, then sautéed to tender perfection and served with a buttery peppercorn sauce. It is my version of a favourite dish sampled and very much enjoyed at the Old Angler's Inn in Potomac, Maryland, USA.

Place the peppercorns with their brine, the honey, olive oil and black pepper to taste in a blender or food processor and purée until smooth. Place the tuna steaks in a shallow dish, pour over the peppercorn mixture, cover and marinate in the refrigerator for 8 hours, turning occasionally.

Drain the tuna steaks, reserving the marinade. Place the marinade in a blender or food processor with the butter and process until well blended. Chill for about 30 minutes.

2 **4** 🌡 2 OVEN RANGE, 4 OVEN RANGE, THERMODIAL-CONTROLLED RANGE: Heat the oil in a large heavy-based frying pan until hot but not smoking, add the tuna steaks and sauté for about 2-3 minutes on each side until cooked but still juicy. Transfer to a cutting board and cut the steaks into thin slices with a knife held at a 45° angle. Arrange the slices in a fan pattern on heated serving plates.

Meanwhile, place the prepared chilled peppercorn butter mixture in a small pan and heat gently over a low heat, whisking constantly, until the mixture has just melted but is still creamy and emulsified. Spoon over the tuna to serve.

SCALLOPS WITH PINK GRAPEFRUIT SAUCE

SERVES 4

675 g (1½ lb) scallops, cut into 1.5 cm (½ inch) slices

2 tablespoons seasoned plain flour

4 tablespoons olive oil

6 tablespoons dry white wine

4 tablespoons canned or bottled clam juice or concentrated fish stock

2 tablespoons minced onion or shallot

150 ml (¼ pint) fresh pink grapefruit juice

1 teaspoon grated pink grapefruit zest

1 teaspoon sugar

75 g (3 oz) unsalted butter

2 tablespoons finely chopped spring onions

2 pink grapefruit, peeled, pith removed and cut into segments, to garnish

I first tried this dish at a very smart and highly fashionable restaurant in San Diego where American or Californian cuisine was all the rage. Served with a cornucopia of colourful baby vegetables and roasted sliced potatoes seasoned with rosemary, it was a memorable meal and here is my version of the main dish. Do remember when adding the butter not to heat the sauce too much so that it liquefies – it should be gently warmed to produce a sauce the consistency of thin hollandaise.

2 **4** 🌡 2 OVEN RANGE, 4 OVEN RANGE, THERMODIAL-CONTROLLED RANGE: Toss the scallop slices in the seasoned flour to coat. Heat the oil in a large heavy-based frying pan until it is hot but not smoking. Add the scallop slices and sauté for 2½-3 minutes, or until they are just firm and lightly golden. Remove from the pan with a slotted spoon and set aside.

Add the wine to the pan, scraping up any pan sediment, then stir in the clam juice or concentrated fish stock, the shallot, grapefruit juice, zest and sugar, mixing well. Bring to the boil and cook until the mixture is reduced to about 4 tablespoons. Strain through a sieve set over a saucepan.

Place the pan over a gentle heat on the Simmering Plate and whisk in the butter, a small knob at a time, until smooth and creamy, allowing one knob of butter to melt before adding the next. Add the spring onion, mixing well.

Return the scallops to the sauce and cook gently until heated through, about 1 minute. Serve at once, garnished with the pink grapefruit segments.

TIDEWATER CRAB CAKES WITH WATERCRESS MAYONNAISE

SERVES 6

50 g (2 oz) unsalted butter

75 g (3 oz) plain flour

150 ml (¼ pint) milk

½ teaspoon mustard powder

2 egg yolks

4 teaspoons capers, coarsely chopped

pinch of cayenne pepper

salt and pepper

450 g (1 lb) flaked crabmeat

juice of 1 lemon

1 egg, beaten

75 g (3 oz) fresh white breadcrumbs

2 tablespoons vegetable oil

1 bunch watercress, trimmed and finely chopped

250 ml (8 fl oz) lemon mayonnaise

1 tablespoon natural yogurt

lemon wedges, to serve

Erase all memories of shop-bought, bland fish cakes and try this recipe for succulent and crispy patties of fresh crab served sizzling hot from the pan. Serve with wedges of lemon and lashings of watercress mayonnaise.

2 **4** 🌡 2 OVEN RANGE, 4 OVEN RANGE, THERMODIAL-CONTROLLED RANGE: Melt half of the butter in a heavy-based pan. Add 25 g (1 oz) of the flour and cook for 1 minute. Gradually add 6 tablespoons of the milk, bring to the boil, reduce the heat and simmer for 2 minutes, stirring constantly, until smooth and thickened. Remove from the heat and add the mustard, egg yolks, capers, cayenne and salt and pepper to taste, mixing well. Stir in the crabmeat and lemon juice, cover and chill until firm enough to handle.

Divide and shape the crabmeat mixture into 6 patties. Coat in the remaining flour. Mix the egg with the remaining milk. Dip the crabcakes into the egg mixture then into the breadcrumbs to coat. Chill for at least 30 minutes to allow the coating to set.

To cook, heat the remaining butter and oil in a large heavy-based frying pan. Add the crabcakes and sauté until crisp and golden on both sides, about 6 minutes. Drain on absorbent kitchen paper.

Meanwhile to make the watercress mayonnaise, mix the watercress with the mayonnaise, yogurt and salt and pepper to taste.

Serve the crab cakes hot with wedges of lemon and the watercress mayonnaise.

HALIBUT IN A TURBAN

This is my husband's name for halibut baked with a lemon curry sauce and even though the sauce isn't Indian it does have a somewhat eastern masala-like texture and flavour. I've always thought that halibut should be treated more like meat than fish since it does have a meaty texture and this robust treatment works very well.

SERVES 6

250 ml (8 fl oz) mayonnaise

250 ml (8 fl oz) soured cream

3 tablespoons dry sherry

¼-½ teaspoon curry powder
(according to taste)

2 tablespoons lemon juice

1 small onion, thinly sliced

900 g (2 lb) halibut fillet pieces
or 6 thick halibut steaks

parsley sprigs, to garnish

Mix the mayonnaise with the soured cream, sherry, curry powder and lemon juice. Sprinkle the sliced onion in a large baking dish and arrange the halibut on top. Spread the prepared sauce evenly over the halibut.

2 2 OVEN RANGE: Cook the halibut in the Roasting Oven with the grid shelf on the second set of runners and the cold plain shelf above for 30-35 minutes or until the fish just flakes.

4 4 OVEN RANGE: Cook in the Baking Oven with the grid shelf on the third set of runners for 30-35 minutes or until the fish flakes.

 THERMODIAL-CONTROLLED RANGE: Cook in the oven set at 180°C/350°F for 30-35 minutes or until the fish flakes.

Serve the halibut hot, garnished with parsley sprigs.

MEAT

ROAST BEEF, VEAL, LAMB AND PORK

Meat roasted in the range cooker is tender, flavoursome and succulent whether you are using the very best cuts or the more economical slow-cooking coarser cuts. Most manufacturers supply a roasting tin that hangs directly from the runners in the oven so you don't need a shelf – take advantage of this facility.

Meat cooked range-style often has minimum shrinkage and rarely requires any additional fat for cooking. There are, like traditional oven cooking, two basic methods to choose from – quick or normal roasting and slow roasting. Quick or normal roasting is better for superior cuts and slow roasting for coarser cuts. Remember to leave roasts to stand after cooking to allow the juices to settle and the muscles to relax – it will make carving so much easier. Do this on the Warming Plate, in the Simmering/Warming Oven or under a tent of foil to keep in the heat.

QUICK ROASTING

2 **4** 2 OVEN RANGE AND 4 OVEN RANGE: Trim the meat if necessary and tie to a neat shape if required. Season to taste with salt and pepper and place in a roasting tin. Hang the tin on the lowest set of runners in the Roasting Oven and cook for the recommended quick/normal roasting time per 450 g (1 lb). Check frequently towards the end of the cooking time since cooking times for joints of the same weight will vary slightly depending upon their size and shape (a smaller narrower joint for example will cook slightly faster than a more solid even-shaped joint). Remove from the oven and leave to stand for 15 minutes before carving.

SLOW ROASTING

2 **4** 2 OVEN RANGE AND 4 OVEN RANGE: Prepare as above and cook in the Roasting Oven for the first 30 minutes of the calculated cooking time. Transfer to the Simmering Oven for *TWICE* the remaining calculated cooking time. Return to the Roasting Oven to crisp just before the end of cooking if you prefer. The exception is less tender beef roasts like brisket and silverside which should be slow roasted for 1 hour per 450 g (1 lb) in the Simmering Oven after being transferred from the Roasting Oven.

TYPE	COOKING TIME PER 450 g (1 lb)
Beef – rare on the bone	10-11 minutes
– rare off the bone	13 minutes
– medium/rare on the bone	12 minutes
– medium/rare off the bone	15 minutes
– medium/well done on the bone	13-14 minutes
– medium/well done off the bone	17-18 minutes
– well done on the bone	17 minutes
– well done off the bone	19-20 minutes
– fillet	10 minutes
Veal	20 minutes
Lamb – pink	15 minutes
– medium/well done	20 minutes
Pork	25 minutes

THERMODIAL-CONTROLLED RANGE: Prepare the joint as above and place in the roasting tin. Cook in the oven set at the recommended temperature and roast for the recommended cooking time per 450 g (1 lb). Leave to stand for 15 minutes before carving.

QUICK ROASTING

Set the oven temperature to 190-200°C/375-400°F:

TYPE	COOKING TIME
Beef – medium	15 minutes per 450 g (1 lb) plus 15 minutes
Veal	18 minutes per 450 g (1 lb) plus 20 minutes
Lamb – pink	15 minutes per 450 g (1 lb) plus 15 minutes
– medium/well done	20 minutes per 450 g (1 lb) plus 20 minutes
Pork	25-30 minutes per 450 g (1 lb) plus 30 minutes

SLOW ROASTING

Set the oven temperature to 150-180°C/300-350°F:

TYPE	COOKING TIME
Beef	25 minutes per 450 g (1 lb) plus 25 minutes
Veal	30-35 minutes per 450 g (1 lb) plus 30 minutes
Lamb	35 minutes per 450 g (1 lb) plus 35 minutes
Pork	35 minutes per 450 g (1 lb) plus 35 minutes

YORKSHIRE PUDDINGS

SERVES 4-6

100 g (4 oz) plain flour

pinch of salt

1 egg

300 ml (½ pint) milk or milk
and water mixed

a little white fat, lard or
dripping

I've been making Yorkshire puddings since I was seven. It was the first thing my mother taught me to make – hardly surprising since I have a Yorkshire father and we were living in Yorkshire at the time. Everyone had their own 'secret' for making the pudding rise to unrivalled heights. My mother added a tablespoon of hot water to the batter just before cooking, my grandmother insisted that the batter had to stand for at least 30 minutes before baking. I think it is just a question of getting the oven temperature right and of giving the pudding a good beating while mixing. My son Charles, with some obvious Yorkshire genes in his makeup, loves Yorkshire pudding and insists that we have it with roast lamb, pork, chicken as well as beef. Purists may be alarmed but it does taste surprisingly good.

Sift the flour and salt into a bowl. Make a well in the centre, crack in the egg and gradually draw the flour into the egg by beating with a wooden spoon. Gradually add the milk or milk and water mixture while doing this until all the flour and milk has been incorporated and you have a smooth creamy mixture. Beat very well for a few minutes.

Place a little fat, lard or dripping in the bases of a 12 hole deep patty tin tray, 2 x 4 hole Yorkshire pudding trays or a small roasting tin.

2 OVEN RANGE AND 4 OVEN RANGE: Place the chosen tin or tins in the Roasting Oven with the grid shelf on the second set of runners and heat until the fat has melted and the tins are very hot. Remove from the oven and pour in the prepared batter. Return to the oven and cook until crisp, brown and well-risen. Small 12 patty Yorkshire puddings will take about 15 minutes, 4 hole Yorkshire puddings will take about 25-30 minutes and a large whole pudding cooked in a small roasting tin will take about 35-40 minutes.

THERMODIAL-CONTROLLED RANGE: Place the chosen tin or tins in the oven set at 220°C/425°F and heat until the fat has melted and the tins are very hot. Remove from the oven and pour in the prepared batter. Return to the oven and cook until crisp, brown and well-risen. Small 12 patty Yorkshire puddings will take about 15 minutes, 4 hole Yorkshire puddings will take about 20-30 minutes and a large whole pudding cooked in a small roasting tin will take about 30-40 minutes.

Serve at once, straight from the oven with roast meats.

STEAK AND KIDNEY HOT POT

SERVES 4

25 g (1 oz) plain flour

2 teaspoons mustard powder

2 teaspoons salt

½ teaspoon ground black pepper

450 g (1 lb) stewing steak, cut into 2.5. cm (1 inch) cubes

8 lamb's kidneys, skinned, halved and cored

2 tablespoons oil

1 large onion, chopped

2 small swedes, peeled and quartered

4 small carrots, peeled and quartered

300 ml (½ pint) beer or beef stock

100 g (4 oz) mushrooms

chopped parsley, to garnish

 Here is a tasty and economical way to fill and satisfy the family during the cold winter months – a hale and hearty, traditional hot pot spiced up and fired with mustard. If you like the mixture can be topped with puff pastry to make a wonderful pie.

Mix the flour, mustard powder, salt and pepper in a large bag and shake to mix. Add the steak and kidney and toss well to coat the meat on all sides.

Heat the oil in a large casserole on the Boiling Plate, add the meat and cook until browned. Add the onion and cook until softened. Add the swedes, carrots and any remaining flour and mix well. Add the beer or beef stock and stir well to blend. Bring to the boil, transfer to the Simmering Plate and cook for 5 minutes.

2 **4** 2 OVEN RANGE AND 4 OVEN RANGE: Transfer to the floor of the Simmering Oven and cook for 2½ hours. Add the mushrooms, mixing well and cook for a further 30 minutes.

THERMODIAL-CONTROLLED RANGE: Transfer to the oven set at 160°C/325°F and cook for 1½ hours. Add the mushrooms, mixing well and cook for a further 45-60 minutes.

Serve hot, straight from the oven, sprinkled with chopped parsley.

VARIATION

STEAK AND KIDNEY HOT POT WITH A GOLDEN CRUST: Transfer the hot pot mixture to a large pie dish and place a pie funnel in the centre. Roll out 400 g (14 oz) defrosted frozen puff pastry on a lightly floured surface to about 5 cm (2 inches) larger than the top of the pie dish. Cut a 2.5 cm (1 inch) strip from around the pastry, dampen with water and fix to the pie dish rim. Brush again with water. Top with the pastry crust, trim, seal and flute the edges. Use any pastry trimmings to decorate the pie and glaze the whole with beaten egg.

2 **4** 2 OVEN RANGE AND 4 OVEN RANGE: Place in the Roasting Oven with grid shelf on the 2nd or 3rd set of runners and cook for 25-30 minutes or until well-risen, crisp and golden.

THERMODIAL-CONTROLLED RANGE: Cook in the oven set at 220°C/425°F for 25-30 minutes or until well-risen, crisp and golden.

CHILLI BEEF PITTAS

MAKES 8

450 g (1 lb) lean minced beef or steak

1 clove garlic, crushed

1 x 400 g (14 oz) can kidney beans, drained and coarsely chopped

2 teaspoons mild chilli powder

salt and pepper

To serve

pitta bread

relishes

salad leaves

tomato slices

Here is a superior alternative to the plain hamburger in a bun – a spicy beef and chilli bean burger all the better for serving with salad and relishes in a pitta bread. Eat your heart out MacDonalds!

Mix the beef with the garlic, kidney beans, chilli powder and salt and pepper to taste, blending well. Divide the mixture into eight portions then press each into a flat hamburger shape. Place on a baking sheet.

 2 OVEN RANGE AND 4 OVEN RANGE: Cook in the Roasting Oven with the grid shelf on the oven floor for about 10-12 minutes, or until cooked.

THERMODIAL-CONTROLLED RANGE: Cook in the oven set at 200°C/ 400°F for 10-12 minutes or until cooked.

Allow to cool slightly then serve hot or cold in pitta bread 'pockets' with salad leaves, tomato slices and relishes of your choice.

BEEF DAUBE

SERVES 6-8

2 tablespoons olive oil

1 large onion or 8 shallots

2 celery stalks, chopped into 2.5 cm (1 inch) lengths

1.125 kg (2½ lb) lean braising steak

50 g (2 oz) plain flour

salt and pepper

600 ml (1 pint) beef stock

2 cloves garlic, crushed

150 ml (¼ pint) red wine

2 tablespoons red wine vinegar

1 tablespoon tomato purée

2 tablespoons snipped chives

1 teaspoon chopped fresh thyme

2 bay leaves

450 g (1 lb) parsnips, peeled and cut into bite-sized pieces

225 g (8 oz) mushrooms

 A wonderfully easy main course dish that can be made well ahead and left to cook while you enjoy time with friends or family. Deceptively homely it can also be made to look very smart if you use small whole shallots instead of a large whole onion; add a few dried (soaked according to packet instructions) or canned whole chestnuts; or include a few baby turnips instead of a few of the parsnips to the basic mixture.

Heat the oil in a large heavy-based frying pan on the Boiling Plate. Cut the large onion into wedges or leave the shallots whole. Add to the pan and fry quickly until browned on all sides. Remove with a slotted spoon and place in a large casserole. Add the celery and cook for about 3-4 minutes until lightly browned and softened. Transfer to the casserole.

Cut the meat into large pieces and coat in the flour seasoned with a little salt and pepper. Add to the pan and sauté until browned on both sides. Transfer to the casserole. Add the stock, garlic, wine, vinegar, tomato purée, chives and thyme to the pan and heat gently, scraping up any sediment. Pour over the meat and vegetable mixture then tuck in the bay leaves.

2 **4** 2 OVEN RANGE AND 4 OVEN RANGE: Cover and cook on the Simmering Plate for 10 minutes. Transfer to the Simmering Oven floor on a grid shelf and cook for 1 hour. Remove the casserole from the oven, add the parsnips and mushrooms, mixing well. Re-cover, return to the oven and cook for a further 2-2½ hours until the meat and vegetables are very tender.

THERMODIAL-CONTROLLED RANGE: Cover and cook on the Simmering Plate for 10 minutes. Transfer to the oven set at 160°C/325°F and cook for 1 hour. Remove the casserole from the oven, add the parsnips and mushrooms, mixing well. Re-cover, return to the oven and cook for a further 1½-2 hours until the meat and vegetables are very tender. Alternatively, cook in the Simmering Oven all day or overnight or for 6-8 hours until tender.

VARIATION

DAUBE WITH DUMPLINGS: Sift 175 g (6 oz) self-raising flour into a bowl. Add salt and pepper to taste, 1 tablespoon chopped mixed herbs (optional) and 75 g (3 oz) suet. Stir in enough cold water to make a soft dough. Divide into 8 balls and dust in a little flour. Place on top of the meat and vegetable daube about 20 minutes before the end of the cooking time. Re-cover and cook until well-risen and fluffy.

THE VERY BEST SPAGHETTI BOLOGNESE

SERVES 6

675 g (1½ lb) lean minced beef or steak

2 large Spanish onions, chopped

2 x 400 g (14 oz) cans or cartons passata

2 beef stock cubes, crumbled

dash of Worcestershire sauce

1 tablespoon chopped fresh mixed herbs (parsley, basil and thyme, for example)

salt and pepper

My children and many of their friends, who visit on a regular basis after school with voracious appetites, enjoy pasta with a bolognese sauce. So popular is this dish that it is a regular weekly favourite cooked in my Aga. The recipe has changed over the years and has been adapted recently to include passata or creamed tomatoes to give a really thick tomato flavour to the sauce. I hope like me that you will find it a wonderfully versatile recipe – I use the basic mixture with a béchamel cheese sauce and sheet pasta to make lasagne and add chilli powder and canned red kidney beans to the base to make chilli con carne.

Place the minced beef or steak in a large, heavy-based covered pan or casserole and cook on the Boiling Plate to brown quickly, stirring frequently to break up. Drain away any excess fat. Add the onions, passata, stock cubes, Worcestershire sauce, herbs and salt and pepper to taste, mixing well. Bring to the boil, transfer to the Simmering Plate, cover and cook for about 10 minutes.

  2 OVEN RANGE AND 4 OVEN RANGE: Transfer to the Simmering Oven and cook for 1½-1¾ hours.

THERMODIAL-CONTROLLED RANGE: Transfer to the oven set at 160°C/325°F and cook for 1½ hours.

Serve with cooked spaghetti or pasta (cook about 50 g/2 oz dried pasta per portion for average appetites) and sprinkled with grated Parmesan cheese.

VARIATIONS

CHILLI CON CARNE: Prepare and cook as above but add 1 tablespoon chilli seasoning and 1 x 400 g (14 oz) can red kidney beans. Serve with cooked rice and salad.

LASAGNE: Prepare and cook the sauce as above then layer with 300 ml (½ pint) thick cheese sauce and 175 g (6 oz) lasagne in a large, shallow ovenproof dish, finishing with a layer of cheese sauce. Sprinkle with grated Parmesan cheese and bake in the Roasting Oven with the grid shelf on the floor of the oven for about 30-35 minutes or with the oven set at 200°C/400°F for about 25-30 minutes or until golden brown. Serve with a crisp seasonal salad.

FILLET OF BEEF WITH GRAND MARNIER AND MUSHROOM SAUCE

SERVES 6

24 shallots

50 g (2 oz) butter

225 g (8 oz) Shitake mushrooms, sliced

2 cloves garlic, crushed

6 tablespoons dry white wine

4 tablespoons Grand Marnier

600 ml (1 pint) beef stock

1 bouquet garni (tied in a piece of cheesecloth or muslin)

1 tablespoon tomato paste

3 tablespoons sugar

3 tablespoons red wine vinegar

6 tablespoons orange juice

4 teaspoons arrowroot powder dissolved in 2 tablespoons Grand Marnier

lemon juice, to taste

1 tablespoon oil

1.125-1.35 kg (2½-3 lb) beef fillet

salt and pepper

Every now and then I splash out and buy a fillet of beef for a special occasion, usually when the purse strings and my bank manager are behaving in an unusually relaxed fashion! A special cut of meat deserves a special sauce and this one is equally as extravagant with Shitake mushrooms and Grand Marnier as the principle flavouring agents. All in all a doubly delicious experience.

Place the shallots in a large pan with half of the butter and cook until golden. Add the mushrooms and cook, stirring constantly, for 5 minutes. Add the garlic and cook, stirring constantly, for 1 minute. Add the wine and Grand Marnier and boil for 1 minute. Add the stock, bouquet garni and tomato paste, mixing well. Simmer for 30 minutes.

Place the sugar and red wine vinegar in a small pan and cook until the mixture is syrupy then stir in the orange juice. Cook, stirring constantly, until the caramel is dissolved then add to the sauce mixture. Bring the sauce to the boil, stir in the dissolved arrowroot and simmer, stirring constantly, until thickened. Remove and discard the bouquet garni. Add the lemon juice and salt and pepper to taste. Keep warm while cooking the beef fillet.

Melt the remaining butter with the oil in a large frying pan, add the beef fillet, season with salt and pepper and sauté until browned on all sides. Transfer to a roasting tin.

2 | 4 2 OVEN RANGE AND 4 OVEN RANGE: Cook the beef in the Roasting Oven with the grid shelf on the highest set of runners until cooked to your liking. Allow about 15 minutes for rare beef and about 18 minutes for medium beef (cooking time will depend very much upon the thickness of the beef fillet, sautéeing time and the temperature of the Roasting Oven).

THERMODIAL-CONTROLLED RANGE: Cook the beef in the oven set at 230°C/450°F until cooked to your liking. Allow about 15 minutes for rare beef and about 18 minutes for medium beef (cooking time will depend upon the thickness of the beef fillet, sautéeing time and whether the oven is up to temperature).

Allow to stand for 5 minutes before slicing to serve with the sauce.

GREEK MOUSSAKA

SERVES 6

3 tablespoons oil

450 g (1 lb) aubergines, thinly sliced

2 onions, sliced

1 clove garlic, crushed

450 g (1 lb) lean minced lamb or ½ shoulder lamb, boned and minced

50 g (2 oz) mushrooms, chopped

1 x 400 g (14 oz) can chopped tomatoes

1 tablespoon tomato purée

salt and pepper

Topping

2 eggs

150 ml (¼ pint) single cream or top of the milk

75 g (3 oz) Cheddar or Parmesan cheese, grated

 I always used to think moussaka was something of a chore to make because it was difficult to find raw minced lamb. Now it seems that every supermarket in the land stocks the basic ingredient and it is so quick to make and assemble. Everyone has their favourite recipe – this is mine. If you want a lighter and healthier dish then blanch the aubergine slices rather than frying them.

Heat half of the oil in a large frying pan, add some of the aubergine slices and fry gently until softened, about 2-3 minutes, then drain on absorbent kitchen paper. Add a little more of the oil and continue to fry the aubergine slices and drain as before. Alternatively, blanch in a pan of boiling water for 1 minute then drain thoroughly.

Add the onion and garlic to the pan and cook on the Simmering Plate for about 5-10 minutes until softened. Add the lamb and mushrooms and fry for about 10 minutes, stirring frequently to break up. Stir in the tomatoes, tomato purée and salt and pepper to taste. Bring to the boil on the Boiling Plate then transfer to the Simmering Plate and cook for 20 minutes.

To assemble, put half of the meat mixture in a large, shallow, greased ovenproof dish and cover with half of the aubergines. Repeat with the remaining lamb and aubergines.

2 **4** 2 OVEN RANGE AND 4 OVEN RANGE: Place in the Roasting Oven with the grid shelf on the floor of the oven and cook uncovered for about 20 minutes. Beat all the topping ingredients together and pour over the top of the baked mixture. Return to the oven and cook for a further 10-15 minutes until golden brown.

THERMODIAL-CONTROLLED RANGE: Place in the oven set at 180°C/ 350°F and bake uncovered for 30 minutes. Beat all the topping ingredients together and pour over the baked mixture. Return to the oven and cook for a further 15-20 minutes until golden brown.

TEXAN BARBECUED LEG OF LAMB WITH RICE

SERVES 6

1 x 2.25 kg (5 lb) leg of lamb

Marinade

2 teaspoons mustard powder

2 teaspoons chilli powder

300 ml (½ pint) water

300 ml (½ pint) fresh orange juice

300 ml (½ pint) red wine

4 cloves garlic, crushed

4 tablespoons brown sugar

225 g (8 oz) long-grain rice

4 tablespoons chopped parsley

2 oranges, segmented and chopped

orange slices and watercress sprigs, to garnish

 This is a really tasty dish where the leg of lamb is marinaded in a red wine, orange juice and spice mixture then the marinade is used to cook the accompanying rice. The dish needs little more than a crisp salad accompaniment.

Place the lamb in a shallow dish. Mix the mustard powder with the chilli powder, water, orange juice, red wine, garlic and brown sugar. Pour over the meat and coat well. Cover and chill for 12-24 hours, turning occasionally.

Drain the lamb from the marinade and place on a rack in a roasting tin. Remove and reserve 350 ml (12 fl oz) of the marinade for cooking the rice.

2 4 2 OVEN RANGE AND 4 OVEN RANGE: Cook in the Roasting Oven with the roasting tin hung on the lowest set of runners or with the grid shelf on the floor of the oven for 1¼ hours if you like your lamb pink or 1 hour 40 minutes if you prefer your lamb medium to well done, basting occasionally with the marinade. Remove to the Simmering Oven and leave to stand for 15 minutes so that the lamb is easier to carve.

THERMODIAL-CONTROLLED RANGE: Cook in the oven set at 180°C/350°F for 2-2½ hours until the meat is cooked according to taste, basting occasionally with the marinade.

About 20 minutes before you intend to serve the lamb, wash the rice and place in a large flameproof casserole with the reserved marinade. Bring to the boil, stir well and cover.

2 4 2 OVEN RANGE AND 4 OVEN RANGE: Transfer the casserole to the floor of the Simmering Oven and allow to cook for 15-20 minutes or until the rice is cooked and has absorbed all of the marinade. Add the parsley and chopped orange segments, mixing well.

THERMODIAL-CONTROLLED RANGE: Transfer the casserole to the oven floor and allow the rice to cook with the lamb for 20 minutes or until it is cooked and has absorbed all of the marinade. Add the parsley and chopped orange segments, mixing well.

Serve the lamb garnished with orange slices and watercress sprigs and with the hot cooked rice.

LIME AND CORIANDER LAMB KEBABS

SERVES 4

175 g (6 oz) set natural yogurt

4 cloves garlic, crushed

grated rind and juice of 1 lime

1 teaspoon ground turmeric

1 teaspoon clear honey

1 tablespoon oil

2 tablespoons chopped fresh coriander

salt and pepper

675 g (1½ lb) lamb neck fillet, cut into bite-size pieces or cubes

2 limes, each cut into 4 wedges

When the weather turns unpredictable and an outdoor barbecue looks doomed then use the range to produce a barbecue-style meal. A cast-iron ridged grill pan will give authentic-looking and tasting barbecue fare from steaks and sausages to chops and, of course, kebabs. The lamb kebabs here are coated in a Turkish-inspired marinade made from yogurt, garlic, lime, honey, turmeric and fresh coriander. Serve with brown rice or in a pitta bread with salad.

2 **4** **🌡** 2 OVEN RANGE, 4 OVEN RANGE, THERMODIAL-CONTROLLED RANGE: In a large bowl, mix the yogurt with the garlic, lime rind and juice, turmeric, honey, oil, coriander and salt and pepper to taste. Add the meat and stir well to ensure that the meat is evenly coated. Cover and leave to marinate in the refrigerator for 3-4 hours or overnight.

Thread the meat and lime segments onto 4 metal skewers. Heat a cast-iron ridged grill pan on the Boiling Plate until hot. Add the kebabs and immediately transfer to the Simmering Plate. Cook over a gentle to moderate heat for about 10-12 minutes, turning and basting frequently with the remaining marinade until tender.

VEAL CHOPS WITH AUBERGINE STUFFING AND ROASTED RED PEPPER SAUCE

SERVES 4

4 rib veal chops, cut about 2.5 cm (1 inch) thick

2 tablespoons vegetable oil

Stuffing

1 onion, minced

2 tablespoons olive oil

3 cloves garlic, crushed

What could be more enticing than tender veal chops stuffed with a tasty aubergine and yellow pepper mixture served with rich and vibrant red pepper sauce? Serve it with sautéed baby artichokes and the tiniest new potatoes.

To make the stuffing, place the onion and oil in a large frying pan and cook until softened, about 5 minutes. Add the garlic, yellow peppers and aubergine and cook, stirring occasionally, for 6-8 minutes, or until the aubergine is softened. Stir in the tomatoes, herbes de Provence, sage, basil, parsley, salt and black pepper to taste. Cook, stirring constantly, for 1 minute then remove from the heat and allow to cool.

2 yellow peppers, cored, seeded and chopped
1 aubergine, weighing about 225 g (8 oz), peeled and chopped
2 tomatoes, peeled, seeded and chopped
2 teaspoons dried herbes de Provence
½ teaspoon dried sage
½ teaspoon dried basil
1 tablespoon chopped fresh parsley
1 teaspoon salt
freshly ground black pepper
Sauce
2 large red peppers, roasted, peeled and chopped
4 tablespoons extra virgin olive oil
1½ teaspoons lemon juice
1½ teaspoons balsamic vinegar
cayenne pepper, to taste
1 tablespoon water
chopped parsley, to garnish

Trim the fat away from the narrow end bones of the chops. With a sharp knife make a cut along the fat side of each chop to make a pocket to hold the stuffing. Stuff each chop with an equal quantity of the stuffing and secure the pockets with wooden cocktail sticks. Brush with the oil and place in a roasting tin.

2 **4** 2 OVEN RANGE AND 4 OVEN RANGE: Cook the chops in the Roasting Oven on the oven floor for about 8-10 minutes each side, or until they are cooked through but the flesh is slightly pink near the bone, basting halfway through the cooking time with any pan juices. Remove from the oven and allow to stand for 3 minutes.

THERMODIAL-CONTROLLED RANGE: Cook the chops in the oven set at 230°C/450°F on the oven floor for about 8-10 minutes each side, or until they are cooked through but the flesh is still slightly pink near the bone, basting halfway through the cooking time with any pan juices. Remove from the oven and allow to stand for 3 minutes.

Meanwhile, to make the sauce, place the roasted peppers in a food processor or blender with the oil, lemon juice, vinegar, cayenne pepper, water and salt and pepper to taste. Purée until smooth.

To serve, remove and discard the wooden cocktail sticks from the chops and arrange on heated serving plates. Pour some of the sauce around each chop and sprinkle with chopped parsley.

ROAST PORK WITH CRANBERRY AND HERB STUFFING

SERVES 4-6

1 onion, finely chopped

50 g (2 oz) fresh cranberries, chopped

grated rind and juice of 1 orange

75 g (3 oz) fresh breadcrumbs

1 tablespoon chopped fresh sage

1 tablespoon chopped parsley

salt and pepper

1 x 1.35 kg (3 lb) boneless pork loin joint

oil

 Pork, roasted with a flavoursome cranberry and herb stuffing makes a welcome change to turkey at Christmas or for winter-time celebratory eating.

Serve with roast potatoes, fresh vegetables and an apple or cranberry sauce.

To make the stuffing, mix the onion with the cranberries, orange rind and juice, breadcrumbs, sage, parsley and salt and pepper to taste. Pack the stuffing into the pork cavity left by the bone and secure with string. Brush the scored rind with a little oil and rub with salt. Weigh the joint to calculate the cooking time then place in a roasting tin.

2 **4** 2 OVEN RANGE AND 4 OVEN RANGE: Cook the joint in the Roasting Oven for 30 minutes. Transfer to the Simmering Oven and cook for *TWICE* the remaining calculated cooking time (see page 60), about 1¾ hours. Return to the Roasting Oven to crisp just before the end of cooking if liked.

THERMODIAL-CONTROLLED RANGE: Cook the joint in the oven set at 150-180°C/300-350°F for 35 minutes per 450 g (1 lb) plus 35 minutes, about 2¼-2½ hours. Raise the oven temperature towards the end of cooking to crisp the skin if liked.

Leave to stand, under foil, for about 10-15 minutes before carving.

PORK AND ORANGE KEDGEREE

SERVES 4

225 g (8 oz) long-grain rice

175 ml (6 fl oz) water

175 ml (6 fl oz) orange juice

salt and pepper

1 tablespoon oil

350 g (12 oz) pork tenderloin, cut into thin strips

4 rashers smoked streaky bacon, rinded and chopped

1 yellow pepper, cored, seeded and chopped

1 teaspoon grated orange zest

2 hard-boiled eggs, shelled and chopped

100 g (4 oz) cooked peas

Today's pork is leaner, tastier and more versatile than it ever has been and in this recipe it is combined with bacon, rice, peppers, hard-boiled eggs and peas and flavoured with orange to make a good supper or lunch dish. It is also a good dish to prepare for healthy appetites for a brunch-style meal.

Place the rice in a large flameproof casserole with the water, orange juice and ½ teaspoon salt. Bring to the boil and cover.

2 **4** 2 OVEN RANGE AND 4 OVEN RANGE: Transfer to the floor of the Simmering Oven and cook for 15-20 minutes or until tender. Alternatively, cook on the Simmering Plate for 15-20 minutes or until tender.

THERMODIAL-CONTROLLED RANGE: Transfer to the oven set at 160°/ 325°F and cook for 15-20 minutes or until tender. Alternatively, cook on the Simmering Plate for 15-20 minutes or until tender.

Drain well and rinse under cold water.

Heat the oil in a large heavy-based frying pan, add the pork and bacon and cook until browned on all sides, about 5 minutes. Add the pepper and cook for a further 2-3 minutes.

Stir in the rice, orange zest, egg and peas with salt and pepper to taste, mixing well. Heat through gently on the Simmering Plate until hot. Serve at once.

CLOCKWATCHER'S LEMON PORK

SERVES 4

2 teaspoons oil

450 g (1 lb) pork tenderloin, cut into 1.5 cm (½ inch) slices

salt and pepper

grated rind of 2 small lemons

juice of 4 small lemons

5 cm (2 inch) piece root ginger, peeled and grated

4 tablespoons dry sherry

2 tablespoons light soy sauce

2 tablespoons clear honey

2 teaspoons cornflour

1 large bunch spring onions, trimmed and chopped

If, like me, more than once in a while you race in from work, a meeting, a school function or from a generally chaotic day out and have to prepare a meal in minutes then this is the dish for you. From start to finish this delicious lemony pork dish takes no more than 10 minutes to cook and served with rice, noodles and salad tastes as if you've been labouring for hours!

2 **4** 2 OVEN RANGE, 4 OVEN RANGE, THERMODIAL-CONTROLLED RANGE: Lightly brush the bottom of a large heavy-based frying pan with the oil. Heat until hot, season the pork with salt and pepper then add to the pan and brown quickly on both sides.

Mix the lemon rind with the lemon juice, ginger, sherry, soy sauce, honey and cornflour. Transfer the pork to the Simmering Plate over a gentle heat and pour over the lemon mixture, stirring constantly. Add the spring onions and simmer, uncovered for about 5 minutes, stirring occasionally.

Serve with rice or noodles and a crisp seasonal salad.

BOILED BACON, GAMMON AND HAM

A cold or hot buffet table spread rarely seems complete without a shiny glazed joint of bacon, ham or gammon studded with cloves. Perfect for serving hot with an onion or mustard sauce or cold with home-made pickles, it is always so enjoyable. Many people prefer to cook the joint on the hob but I have also enjoyed considerable success in the oven. Choose the method you prefer but do remember to cook slowly to ensure tenderness and minimum shrinkage.

2 4 2 OVEN RANGE AND 4 OVEN RANGE: Soak the joint in cold water overnight or for at least 8 hours. Place in a large pan on an upturned plate or small trivet (to prevent the bottom from immediate contact with the pan which can cause scorching) and cover with cold water. Cover and bring slowly to the boil then simmer for 20 minutes per 450 g (1 lb) plus 20 minutes, topping up the water level when necessary. Flavourings can be added at the beginning of cooking to enhance the flavour of the joint (see below).

Alternatively, soak the joint as before and place in a pan on a small upturned plate or trivet and cover with about 7.5 cm (3 inches) cold water. Bring slowly to the boil, cover then simmer for 20 minutes. Add any flavourings then transfer to the floor of the Simmering Oven and cook for the following recommended times.

WEIGHT	COOKING TIME
900 g – 1.35 kg (2-3 lb)	2-2½ hours
1.8 kg – 2.25 kg (4-5 lb)	2½-3 hours
2.7 kg – 3.15 kg (6-7 lb)	3-3½ hours
3.6 kg – 4 kg (8-9 lb)	4-4½ hours
4.5 kg – 5 kg (10-11 lb)	5-5½ hours
5.4 kg – 5.8 kg (12-13 lb)	6-6½ hours
6.3 kg – 6.75 kg (14-15 lb)	7-7½ hours
7.2 kg – 7.6 kg (16-17 lb) plus	at least 8 hours and preferably overnight

THERMODIAL-CONTROLLED RANGE: Soak the joint in cold water overnight or for at least 8 hours. Place in a large pan on an upturned plate or small trivet (to prevent the bottom from immediate contact with the pan which can cause scorching) and cover with cold water. Cover and bring slowly to the boil then simmer for 20 minutes per 450 g (1 lb) plus 20 minutes, topping up the water level when necessary. Flavourings can be added at the beginning of cooking to enhance the flavour of the joint (see below).

Alternatively, soak the joint as before and place in a pan on a small upturned plate or trivet and cover with about 7.5. cm (3 inches) cold water. Bring slowly to the boil, cover then simmer for 20 minutes. Add any flavourings then transfer to the Simmering/Warming Oven or the main oven when the range is on idling heat and cook all day or all night until tender.

SEASONINGS

- Up to half of the liquid can be replaced with cider, apple juice, light beer or a splash or two of wine.

- Sprigs of fresh herbs may be added like sage, rosemary, thyme and 1-2 bay leaves or add a bouquet garni.

- The juice of 1 lemon or 1 orange may be added to the cooking liquid or the same may be sweetened with 1-2 tablespoons honey.

- An onion studded with cloves and 1 large carrot (cut into large pieces) can be added to give flavour.

MARMALADE GLAZED HAM

SERVES ABOUT 20

1 x 5.4 kg (12 lb) cooked ham
(see page 75)

cloves

Glaze

175 g (6 oz) marmalade

75 g (3 oz) honey

1 tablespoon French mustard

grated rind and juice of
2 oranges

I love to have my family to stay at Christmas and simply adore catering on a grand scale during the festivities. On Boxing Day we always have a large buffet for friends and family and the table invariably groans under the weight of a large cooked ham. Some years I boil then bake it with a mustard and sugar glaze but last year, on the recommendation of a friend, I glazed it with this scrummy marmalade mixture.

Prepare and cook the ham as on page 75. Drain and cool the ham slightly then strip off the skin, leaving a thin fatty surface. Score the fat into a diamond pattern with a sharp knife. Press a clove into each alternate diamond and place in a roasting tin.

Mix all the ingredients for the glaze together, heat in a small pan if they are too cold to blend easily. Coat the fat mixture with the glaze, brushing liberally over the surface to coat evenly.

$\boxed{2}\boxed{4}$ 2 OVEN RANGE AND 4 OVEN RANGE: Cook near the top of the Roasting Oven for about 15-20 minutes or until the fat is golden brown, basting 3-4 times with the glaze during this time. Watch and check often, turning the joint so that it browns evenly and the fat does not scorch.

$\boxed{\text{🌡}}$ THERMODIAL-CONTROLLED RANGE: Cook in the oven set at 200°C/400°F for about 15-20 minutes or until the fat is golden brown, basting 3-4 times with the glaze during this time. Watch and check often, turning the joint so that it browns evenly and the fat does not scorch.

VARIATION

Mustard and Brown Sugar Glaze: Mix 175 g (6 oz) soft brown sugar with 4 teaspoons mustard powder, 75 g (3 oz) melted butter, 4 tablespoons cider or apple juice and 2 teaspoons Worcestershire sauce. Use to coat and baste the joint as above.

SMOKED HAM AU GRATIN

This is a tasty dish of smoked ham stuffed with a savoury rice topped with a soured cream gratin mixture. It is good served with a simple sliced tomato salad.

SERVES 4

1 tablespoon oil

1 small onion, finely chopped

100 g (4 oz) long-grain rice

50 g (2 oz) ready-to-eat dried apricots, chopped

300 ml (½ pint) hot vegetable stock

pepper

8 slices smoked ham

1 tablespoon wholegrain mustard

300 ml (½ pint) soured cream

2 tablespoons freshly-grated Parmesan cheese

Heat the oil in a large heavy-based pan, add the onion and cook until tender and golden. Add the rice, apricots and stock, mixing well. Bring to the boil, cover, transfer to the Simmering Plate and cook for about 15 minutes or until the rice has absorbed the stock and is tender. Season with pepper to taste and allow to cool for 2-3 minutes.

Divide the rice mixture between the ham slices, roll up and pack tightly together in a warm shallow ovenproof dish.

Stir the mustard into the soured cream and pour over the ham rolls. Sprinkle with the Parmesan cheese.

$\boxed{2}\boxed{4}$ 2 OVEN RANGE AND 4 OVEN RANGE: Cook in the Roasting Oven on the highest set of runners until a rich golden brown, about 10-15 minutes.

$\boxed{\text{🌡}}$ THERMODIAL-CONTROLLED RANGE: Cook in the top of the oven set at 220-230°C/425-450°F until a rich golden brown, about 10-15 minutes.

CALVES LIVER WITH SAGE AND CARAMELISED ONIONS

SERVES 4

1 large onion

2 tablespoons extra virgin olive oil

15 g (½ oz) butter

450 g (1 lb) calves liver, thinly sliced

freshly ground black pepper

3 sprigs fresh sage, leaves finely chopped

juice of ½ lemon

1 teaspoon balsamic vinegar

 If I have a favourite meal that is cooked in minutes then this has to be it – thin slices of tender calves liver cooked with sage and served with golden caramelised onions and a spoonful or two of pan juices flavoured with lemon juice and fragrant balsamic vinegar.

 2 OVEN RANGE, 4 OVEN RANGE, THERMODIAL-CONTROLLED RANGE: Peel the onion keeping the root end as intact as possible then slice the onion into thin wedges. Heat the oil in a large heavy-based pan, add the onion wedges and fry until a rich golden brown. Remove with a slotted spoon and keep warm.

Add the butter to the pan juices and melt on the Boiling Plate. Season the calves liver with black pepper then add to the pan, a few pieces at a time, and cook quickly on both sides until cooked to your liking. If you like your liver rare and pink on the inside then cook for barely ½ minute on each side, for medium liver cook for about 1 minute on each side. Remove from the pan and keep warm.

Add the lemon juice to the pan juices and stir well to blend. Stir in the vinegar and serve at once with the cooked liver and caramelised onion accompaniment.

LIVER AND POTATO PAN DUO

SERVES 2

1 tablespoon oil

2 large onions, sliced

450 g (1 lb) potatoes, thinly sliced

salt and pepper

75 g (3 oz) sweetcorn kernels

225 g (8 oz) lamb's liver, cut into strips

4 rashers smoked streaky bacon, rinded and chopped

150 ml (¼ pint) natural yogurt

ground paprika, to sprinkle

 Here is a tasty, healthy and economical one pot dish for two. Lamb's liver is combined with smoked streaky bacon, onion, potatoes and sweetcorn for cooking then topped with a yogurt and paprika mixture for serving.

2 OVEN RANGE, 4 OVEN RANGE, THERMODIAL-CONTROLLED RANGE: Brush the oil over the base and sides of a large, heavy-based non-stick deep frying pan. Layer the onions and potatoes in the pan and season with salt and pepper to taste. Sprinkle with the sweetcorn kernels.

Arrange the liver and bacon over the top and cover with a close fitting lid or foil. Cook on the Simmering Plate over a low heat for about 30-40 minutes or until the potato slices are tender.

Remove from the heat, spoon over the yogurt and sprinkle with paprika to serve.

TOAD IN THE HOLE WITH TOMATO AND BASIL SAUCE

I am lucky to have a super butcher nearby with a worthy reputation for producing prize-winning sausages of almost every type from plain beef and pork to herb, garlic, tomato and spiced. This proves a Godsend when making this traditional lunch or supper dish since the sausages are, I think, the all-important ingredient. I have also enjoyed great success with sausages first made and marketed by the great photographer Norman Parkinson, called Porkinsons (now available at many supermarkets and delicatessens throughout the country). Of course the real secret to this dish is to make sure your range is right up to the ideal temperature so that the batter rises beautifully and forms a golden, crunchy crown around the sausages.

Place the sausages in a lightly greased medium roasting tin or baking dish that will take the sausages in one layer and leave sufficient space for the batter to cook and rise.

2 **4** 2 OVEN RANGE AND 4 OVEN RANGE: Place the tin or dish on the grid shelf on the second set of runners in the Roasting Oven and cook for 10 minutes. Place all the sauce ingredients in a small casserole and bring to boiling point on the Boiling Plate. Transfer to the bottom of the Roasting Oven.

To prepare the batter, sift the flour into a bowl with the salt. Gradually stir in the beaten eggs and milk or milk and water mixture and beat to make a smooth batter. Turn the sausages over, pour in the batter and return to the oven for a further 25-30 minutes or until the batter is well-risen, crisp and golden brown.

THERMODIAL-CONTROLLED RANGE: Place the tin or dish in the oven set at 230°C/450°F and cook for 10 minutes. Place all the sauce ingredients in a small casserole and bring to boiling point on the Boiling Plate. Transfer to the bottom of the oven.

To prepare the batter, sift the flour into a bowl with the salt. Gradually stir in the beaten eggs and milk or milk and water mixture and beat to make a smooth batter. Turn the sausages over, pour in the batter and return to the oven for about 25-30 minutes or until the batter is well-risen, crisp and golden brown.

Stir the sauce well to mix and blend the flavours. Serve the cooked toad in the hole in generous slices with the tomato and basil sauce.

POULTRY AND GAME

ROAST CHICKEN, TURKEY AND GAME BIRDS

Chicken, turkey, duck and game birds roasted in a range-style cooker are promisingly crisp and golden on the outside yet tender and succulent inside without a hint of drying out. For best results place the bird on a trivet in the roasting tin so that the bird does not literally stew in its own juices. For medium to large birds cover the breast with fat bacon or a smear of butter and foil to prevent over cooking and browning and lift or remove to brown during the latter stages of the cooking. For all birds there is a normal or quick roasting method and for larger turkey birds there is the optional slow roasting method using the Simmering Oven (so useful at Christmas time – I invariably put a heavyweight turkey in the oven after filling the children's stockings and can enjoy Christmas morning without all the usual stuffing and hustle and bustle of cooking).

NORMAL QUICK ROASTING

2 **4** 2 OVEN RANGE AND 4 OVEN RANGE: Lightly smear the bird with butter, stuff if you like and add any preferred seasonings to the cavity. Cover the breast with foil or bacon fat. Place on a trivet in the roasting tin and hang the tin on the lowest set of runners in the Roasting Oven or on the grid shelf placed on the floor of the Roasting Oven for chicken, turkey, goose and duck but on the middle set of runners in the Roasting Oven for other game birds. Cook for the recommended cooking time (remembering to weigh the bird after stuffing), basting occasionally and removing the foil towards the end of the cooking. When cooked the juices from the thickest part of the thigh should run clear. If they are still tinged pink then cook a little longer and retest.

OPPOSITE:
Texan Barbecued Leg of
Lamb with Rice

BIRD	COOKING TIME
Chicken – 900g (2 lb)	45-50 minutes
– 1.35 kg (3 lb)	1 hour
– 1.8 kg (4 lb)	1½ hours
– 2.25 kg (5 lb)	1½-1¾ hours
Turkey – 3.6-4.5 kg (8-10 lb)	1¾-2 hours
– 4.95-6.75 kg (11-15 lb)	2½ hours
– 7.2-10 kg (16-22 lb)	3 hours
Pheasant	45-50 minutes
Partridge	30-35 minutes
Duck	1-1½ hours
Goose	1½-2 hours
Grouse	30-35 minutes
Woodcock	15 minutes
Snipe	15 minutes
Quail	15 minutes
Pigeon	20-30 minutes

SLOW ROASTING FOR TURKEY

2 **4** 2 OVEN RANGE AND 4 OVEN RANGE: Prepare the turkey as above and place on a grid in the roasting tin, cover with foil and cook on the floor of the Simmering Oven for the following recommended times:

Turkey – 3.6-4.5 kg (8-10 lb)	about 9-10 hours
– 4.95-6.75 kg (11-15 lb)	about 11-12 hours
– 7.2-10 kg (16-22 lb)	about 13-14 hours

Return to the Roasting Oven for the final 15 minutes cooking time to crisp and brown the skin further if you prefer.

THERMODIAL-CONTROLLED RANGE: Lightly smear the bird with butter, stuff and add seasonings to the cavity. Cover the breast with foil or bacon fat. Place on a trivet in the roasting tin and hang the tin on the middle set of runners for small poultry and game birds and from the lowest set of runners for large poultry birds. Cook in the oven set at the recommended temperature for quick or slow roasting and for the recommended time per 450 g (1 lb) (remembering to weigh the birds after stuffing), basting occasionally and removing any foil towards the end of the cooking time. When cooked the juices from the thickest part of the thigh should run clear. If they are still tinged pink then cook a little longer and retest.

OPPOSITE:
Duck and Fennel
Casserole

FAST ROASTING

THERMODIAL-CONTROLLED RANGE: Set the oven temperature to 190-200°C/375-400°F.

BIRD	COOKING TIME
Chicken	15 minutes per 450 g (1 lb) plus 15 minutes
Turkey – up to 5.4 kg (12 lb)	15 minutes per 450 g (1 lb) plus 15 minutes
– over 5.4 kg (12 lb)	cook as above then add a further 12 minutes per 450 g (1 lb)
Pheasant	45-50 minutes total cooking time
Partridge	30-35 minutes total cooking time
Duck	20 minutes per 450 g (1 lb) plus 20 minutes
Goose	20 minutes per 450 g (1 lb) plus 20 minutes
Grouse	30-35 minutes total cooking time
Woodcock	15 minutes total cooking time
Snipe	15 minutes total cooking time
Quail	15 minutes total cooking time
Pigeon	20-30 minutes total cooking time

SLOW ROASTING

THERMODIAL-CONTROLLED RANGE: Set the oven at 150-180°C/300-350°F.

Chicken	25 minutes per 450 g (1 lb) plus 25 minutes
Turkey – up to 5.4 kg (12 lb)	25 minutes per 450 g (1 lb) plus 25 minutes
– over 5.4 kg (12 lb)	cook as above then add a further 12 minutes per 450 g (1 lb)

CHICKEN MERATI

SERVES 2

2 x 100 g (4 oz) boneless
chicken breasts, skinned

½ teaspoon ground coriander

½ teaspoon ground cumin

¼ teaspoon ground paprika

pinch of chilli powder

150 ml (¼ pint) natural yogurt

2 tablespoons chopped fresh
coriander

50 g (2 oz) carrot, peeled

50 g (2 oz) spring onions,
trimmed

50 g (2 oz) fresh pineapple,
peeled and cored

50 g (2 oz) French beans,
trimmed

2 teaspoons oil

1 garlic clove, crushed

40 g (1½ oz) raw long-grain
brown rice, cooked
(see page 104)

25 g (1 oz) salted cashew nuts

Although the oven floor of the Roasting Oven is ideal for shallow frying, the Boiling Plate is better suited to stir frying and so is used for cooking this richly-spiced stir-fried chicken dish. It is highly nutritious with the addition of cooked brown rice and deliciously crisp and colourful when mixed with the vegetables, fruit and nuts.

2 4 🌡 2 OVEN RANGE, 4 OVEN RANGE, THERMODIAL-CONTROLLED RANGE: Slice the chicken breast into small strips. Mix the ground coriander with the cumin, paprika and chilli powder. Add the chicken and toss well to coat. Cover and leave to stand for 15 minutes.

Mix the yogurt with the coriander, cover and chill until required.

Cut the carrot, spring onions and pineapple into thin julienne strips. Blanch the carrot, spring onions and green beans in boiling water for 1 minute to soften slightly. Drain and refresh under cold running water.

Heat the oil and garlic in a large frying pan on the Boiling Plate until hot. Add the chicken pieces, in small batches, and sauté quickly until golden. Remove with a slotted spoon and set aside.

Add the vegetable mixture and stir-fry for 2-3 minutes until tender but still crisp. Add the chicken, pineapple, rice and cashew nuts and stir-fry until hot and well blended, about 1-2 minutes.

Serve at once with the yogurt mixture accompaniment and a green salad.

CHICKEN WITH TARRAGON VINEGAR AND WHITE PORT SAUCE

SERVES 4

25 g (1 oz) butter

2 tablespoons olive oil

4 chicken supremes with bone in or 1 x 1.8 kg (4 lb) chicken, jointed into 8 pieces

salt and pepper

4 onions, cut into wedges

150 ml (¼ pint) tarragon vinegar

450 ml (¾ pint) white port

3 tablespoons double cream or crème fraîche

cooked tagliatelle or pasta, to serve

fresh tarragon sprigs, to garnish

The French have a name for this style of dish; it is called au vinaigre and is truly delicious. In the original version the chicken is cooked with sherry vinegar and sherry to make a shiny and glossy sauce – here it is cooked with white port and tarragon vinegar to produce the same, but I think with more body and vigour than the original. The recipe responds well to adaptation – use pork instead of chicken, Marsala or Madeira instead of sherry or white port and sherry vinegar or any other herb variation instead of tarragon.

2 **4** 🌡 2 OVEN RANGE, 4 OVEN RANGE, THERMODIAL-CONTROLLED RANGE: Heat the butter and oil in a large, heavy-based frying pan. Add the chicken with seasoning to taste and cook until browned on all sides. Remove from the pan with a slotted spoon. Add the onion wedges and brown quickly on all sides.

Return the chicken to the pan and add the tarragon vinegar and white port, mixing well. Simmer, very gently for about 25 minutes, turning the chicken supremes over occasionally so that they cook evenly in the mixture.

Remove the chicken supremes from the juices, increase the heat so that the sauce reduces slightly and becomes syrupy. Stir in the cream and mix well.

Return the chicken to the pan, coat in the sauce and reheat for about 1 minute.

Serve at once, on a bed of cooked tagliatelle, garnished with fresh sprigs of tarragon.

HONEY AND ORANGE CORN-FED ROAST CHICKEN

SERVES 4-6

3 tablespoons clear honey

1 teaspoon salt

1 teaspoon ground paprika

1 x 1.8 kg (4 lb) corn-fed or free-range roasting chicken

600 ml (1 pint) unsweetened orange juice

finely grated rind of 1 orange

4 spring onions, chopped

1 small green pepper, cored, seeded and chopped

½ teaspoon ground ginger

1 teaspoon horseradish sauce

salt and pepper

1 tablespoon cornflour

orange wedges and watercress sprigs, to garnish

 The flavour of many chickens, save free-range, leaves much to be desired so whenever possible I buy a corn-fed type. The skin roasts to a golden colour and the flesh has more than a hint of creaminess. The flavour of course speaks for itself – moist and rich. Here it is coated with a honey and paprika mixture then served with an aromatic orange sauce.

Mix the honey with the salt and paprika and use to coat the skin of the chicken. Place on a trivet in a roasting tin.

  2 OVEN RANGE AND 4 OVEN RANGE: Cook in the Roasting Oven with the roasting tin hung on the lowest set of runners for 1½ hours until cooked and tender.

THERMODIAL-CONTROLLED RANGE: Cook in the oven set at 190-200°C/375-400°F for 1¼-1½ hours until cooked and tender.

Meanwhile, mix the orange juice with the orange rind, spring onions, green pepper, ginger, horseradish sauce, salt and pepper to taste and cornflour. Bring to the boil, stirring constantly until smooth and thickened then simmer for 15 minutes.

Remove the chicken from the roasting pan and place on a heated serving plate. Skim any fat from the roasting juices and discard. Pour the pan juices into the sauce and mix well.

Serve the chicken with the sauce separately and garnished with orange wedges and watercress sprigs.

CHICKEN BREASTS WITH SPECKLED GINGER WINE SAUCE

SERVES 6

6 boneless chicken breasts, skinned

1 tablespoon flour

salt and pepper

40 g (1½ oz) butter

1 tablespoon oil

½ bulb fennel, sliced

5 tablespoons green ginger wine

2 tablespoons white wine or dry white vermouth

3 tablespoons snipped fresh chives

juice of ½ lemon

150 ml (1¼ pint) whipping cream

sprigs of fresh fennel, to garnish

 This is a wonderful dish to make for a mid-week dinner party when time is of the essence. Serve with cooked rice or pasta and a seasonal salad and lavishly garnished with sprigs of fresh fennel.

Beat the chicken breasts between sheets of greaseproof paper or cling film until thin. Season the flour liberally with salt and pepper then use to coat both sides of the chicken breasts.

2 4 🌡 2 OVEN RANGE, 4 OVEN RANGE, THERMODIAL-CONTROLLED RANGE: Heat the butter and oil in a large heavy-based frying pan until sizzling, add the chicken breasts and cook until lightly browned and tender on both sides, about 5-7 minutes. Remove from the pan with a slotted spoon and keep warm.

Add the fennel to the pan juices and fry for 2 minutes, stirring frequently. Stir in the ginger wine and wine or vermouth and cook for 1 minute to reduce slightly. Add the lemon juice and cream and cook, over a gentle heat, stirring constantly, until the sauce thickens slightly. Add the chives and mix well.

To serve, place each chicken breast on a heated serving plate and spoon over a little of the sauce. Garnish with sprigs of fresh fennel and serve at once.

GUINEA FOWL OR POUSSINS WITH ORANGE AND SAGE STUFFING

SERVES 4

2 x 900 g (2 lb) oven-ready guinea fowl or 4 x 450 g (1 lb) oven-ready poussins

olive oil

salt and pepper

3 oranges

100 g (4 oz) thickly sliced bread

1 clove garlic, crushed

1 shallot, finely chopped

½ small bulb fennel or 3 sticks celery, finely chopped

2 tablespoons chopped fresh sage

watercress sprigs, to garnish

 A splendid and stylish dinner party dish – guinea fowl or poussins roasted in olive oil, orange juice and seasonings, then served with a crisp and crunchy orange and sage stuffing accompaniment. For special occasions you could save the orange shells to serve the stuffing in. Prepare as below then pack into half shells and drizzle with olive oil. Bake for the last 10 minutes of the cooking time with the chosen bird.

Place the guinea fowl or poussins in a roasting pan and brush with a little olive oil, sprinkle with salt and pepper to taste and the juice squeezed from one of the oranges.

2 **4** 2 OVEN RANGE AND 4 OVEN RANGE: Cook in the Roasting Oven with the grid shelf on the lowest set of runners and cook the guinea fowl for about 45 minutes and the poussins for about 30-40 minutes, basting occasionally.

THERMODIAL-CONTROLLED RANGE: Cook in the oven set at 190°C/ 375°F for about 45 minutes for the guinea fowl and 30-40 minutes for the poussins, basting occasionally.

Meanwhile, cut the bread into small dice and fry in 3 tablespoons of hot olive oil in a frying pan on the Boiling Plate until golden brown and crisp. Drain on absorbent kitchen paper and keep warm. Peel the two oranges and dice the flesh into a bowl along with any juice. Add the garlic, shallot and fennel or celery to the pan and fry until translucent, about 5 minutes. Add the chopped orange and juice, the sage and salt and pepper to taste. Cook for a further 2 minutes. Remove from the heat, add the croûtons and toss to mix. Serve at once with the cooked guinea fowl or poussins. Garnish with watercress sprigs.

ROAST TURKEY WITH A CHOICE OF STUFFINGS

SERVES 6-8

1 x 4.5 kg (10 lb) turkey

butter

Ginger, Pear and Waterchestnut Stuffing

40 g (1½ oz) butter

1 large onion, chopped

175 g (6 oz) fresh white breadcrumbs

1 x 200 g (7 oz) can waterchestnuts, drained and chopped

4 ripe pears, peeled, cored and chopped

50 g (2 oz) raisins

3 tablespoons chopped stem ginger

1 teaspoon ground ginger

1-2 tablespoons cider vinegar

salt and pepper

Sausagemeat and Pineapple

25 g (1 oz) butter

1 large onion, chopped

1 turkey liver

450 g (1 lb) plain or herbed sausagemeat

200g (7 oz) fresh white breadcrumbs

1 tablespoon chopped fresh thyme

finely grated zest of 1 orange and 1 lemon

1 baby fresh pineapple, peeled, cored and finely chopped

¼ teaspoon ground allspice and ground nutmeg

I don't usually plump for turkey at Christmas, preferring to cook a goose, but when I do, I go overboard with the stuffing. I'm often inspired with American recipes for Thanksgiving that feature turkey stuffed with some of the most original concoctions. Here are two stuffings for turkey both worthy of trying – the first made with ginger, pear and waterchestnuts; and the second made with sausagemeat, citrus fruits and pineapple.

To prepare the Ginger, Pear and Waterchestnut Stuffing, melt the butter in a large pan. Add the onion and cook until golden. Remove from the heat and stir in the breadcrumbs, waterchestnuts, pears, raisins, stem ginger, ground ginger, cider vinegar and salt and pepper to taste, mixing well. Use to stuff the neck cavity of the turkey (any remaining stuffing can be placed in small bun tins and cooked separately to serve with the turkey or rolled into balls and placed on skewers for cooking alongside the turkey for about 20-30 minutes).

To prepare the Sausagemeat and Pineapple Stuffing, melt the butter in a large pan. Add the onion and turkey liver and cook until the onion is softened and the liver is cooked. Remove from the heat and chop the turkey liver with a pair of scissors into small pieces. Add the sausagemeat, breadcrumbs, thyme, fruit zests, pineapple, spices and salt and pepper to taste. Use to stuff the neck cavity of the turkey (any remaining stuffing can be placed in small bun tins and cooked separately to serve with the turkey or rolled into balls, dusted with flour then placed on skewers for cooking alongside the turkey for about 30-40 minutes).

Lightly smear the turkey breast with butter, cover with foil and place on a trivet in a roasting tin.

2 | 4 2 OVEN AND 4 OVEN RANGE: Hang the tin on the lowest set of runners in the Roasting Oven or on the grid shelf on the floor of the Roasting Oven and cook for 2-2¼ hours, basting occasionally and removing the foil towards the end of the cooking time. When cooked the juices from the thickest part of the thigh should run clear.

Alternatively, cook the turkey on the floor of the Simmering Oven for 11-12 hours. Transfer to the Roasting Oven for the final 15 minutes cooking time if liked to crisp and brown the skin further.

THERMODIAL-CONTROLLED RANGE: Weigh the stuffed bird to calculate the cooking time. Cook in the oven set at 190-200°C/375-400°F with the tin hung on the lowest set of runners for 15 minutes per 450 g (1 lb) plus 15 minutes.

Allow the turkey to stand, covered in a tent of foil, for 15 minutes before carving. Serve surrounded with any extra cooked stuffing.

SIMPLY SCRUMPTIOUS MEATLOAF

SERVES 4-6

1 small onion, chopped
1 clove garlic, crushed
1 tablespoon extra-virgin olive oil
1 tomato, peeled, seeded and chopped
¼ teaspoon dried oregano
¼ teaspoon dried basil
1½ tablespoons dry red wine
1 small green pepper, cored, seeded and chopped
1 small courgette, trimmed and finely chopped
20 g (¾ oz) chopped fresh parsley
3 fresh basil leaves, finely chopped
450 g (1 lb) minced raw turkey meat
40 g (1½ oz) fresh white breadcrumbs
½ teaspoon freshly ground white pepper
1 small egg (size 4 or 5), beaten
1 large egg white (size 1 or 2), beaten
salt

 There is a shop in Brooklyn called Simply Scrumptious that sells a wonderful turkey meatloaf. This minced turkey affair is flavoured with onion, garlic, basil, oregano, green peppers, courgettes and red wine. I have persuaded them to share their recipe with you – it is delicious served with fresh seasonal vegetables.

Place half of the onion in a pan with the garlic and oil and cook over a low heat until softened, about 5 minutes. Add the tomato, oregano, basil and wine and simmer for 15 minutes, stirring occasionally.

Place the remaining onion in a food processor or blender with the green pepper and courgette and chop very finely. Mix with the cooked tomato sauce, parsley, basil, turkey, breadcrumbs, pepper, egg, egg white and salt to taste, mixing well. Spoon into a 450 g (1 lb) loaf tin.

2 2 OVEN RANGE: Cook in the Roasting Oven with the grid shelf on the lowest set of runners and the cold plain shelf above for about 1-1¼ hours or until cooked.

4 4 OVEN RANGE: Cook in the Baking Oven with the grid shelf on the second set of runners for about 1¼ hours or until cooked.

 THERMODIAL-CONTROLLED RANGE: Cook in the oven set at 180°C/350°F for about 1¼ hours or until cooked.

Serve hot, cut into slices with fresh seasonal vegetables.

SESAME GLAZED DUCKLING BREASTS WITH VERMOUTH CREAM SAUCE

SERVES 4

4 large duck breast fillets or supremes

1 tablespoon clear honey

1 tablespoon sesame seeds

Sauce

2 tablespoons oil

1 onion, finely chopped

1 tablespoon plain flour

150 ml (¼ pint) well-flavoured chicken stock

4 tablespoons dry white vermouth

1 bay leaf

1 sprig fresh tarragon

salt and pepper

2 tablespoons double cream

 Boneless duckling breast fillets and supremes (partially boned breast portions) are now sold fresh in many supermarkets. They make a good main course dish, are easily prepared and have little or no waste. In the recipe below they are roasted with a drizzle of honey and sprinkling of sesame seeds then served with a creamy vermouth-based sauce. If roasted plain any of the other sauce variations given below can be served for variety.

Rinse and thoroughly dry the duck breasts on absorbent kitchen paper. Place skin-side down in a heavy-based frying pan on the Boiling Plate and cook quickly until the skin is crisp and browned. Remove from the pan and arrange skin-side up on a rack in a small roasting tin. Drizzle over the honey and sprinkle with the sesame seeds.

2 **4** 2 OVEN RANGE AND 4 OVEN RANGE: Roast near the top of the Roasting Oven for 15 minutes until cooked but the flesh is still pink.

 THERMODIAL-CONTROLLED RANGE: Cook in the oven set at 220°C/425°F for about 15 minutes until cooked but the flesh is still pink.

Meanwhile, to make the sauce, heat the oil in a pan, add the onion and cook on the Simmering Plate for about 10 minutes or until softened. Sprinkle in the flour and cook for 1 minute. Remove from the heat and blend in the stock and vermouth. Add the bay leaf, tarragon and salt and pepper to taste. Bring to the boil and simmer for 2 minutes, stirring constantly. Remove from the heat and discard the bay leaf and tarragon. For a smooth sauce, strain through a fine sieve then reheat gently. Stir in the cream and reheat gently.

To serve, cut each breast fillet or the fillet of each supreme diagonally across the grain into thin slices and place fan-like on heated serving plates. Spoon over a little of the sauce and serve at once.

VARIATIONS

Chestnut and Red Wine Sauce: Heat 2 tablespoons oil in a pan, add 1 finely chopped onion and 1 large clove crushed garlic and cook on the Simmering Plate for 10 minutes or until softened and lightly browned. Add 1 tablespoon flour and cook for 1 minute. Remove from the heat and blend in 300 ml (½ pint) well-flavoured chicken stock. Blend 150 ml (¼ pint) red wine a little at a time into 175 g (6 oz) canned chestnut purée to form a smooth paste, then add this to the pan and stir well. Return to the heat, bring to the boil and simmer for 2 minutes, stirring occasionally. Add 2-3 teaspoons soy sauce and pepper to taste. Serve hot with the cooked duck breasts.

Mango and Cognac Sauce: After cooking the duck, skim off any fat from the pan, leaving behind any juices and sediment. Add 4 tablespoons well-flavoured chicken stock and mix well to blend. Add 25 g (1 oz) butter, 2 tablespoons mango chutney, 2 tablespoons orange juice, 2 tablespoons cognac and salt and pepper to taste, mixing well. Blend 1 teaspoon cornflour with a little water and stir into the mixture to thicken. Peel, stone and thinly slice 1 mango, add to the sauce to heat through gently then serve with the cooked duck.

VIETNAMESE BRAISED DUCKLING

SERVES 4

1 x 2 kg (4½ lb) oven-ready duckling

6 dried Chinese mushrooms, soaked in 300 ml (½ pint) water

pared rind of 1 small orange, cut into thin shreds

½ bunch spring onions, finely shredded

1 x 227 g (8 oz) can sliced bamboo shoots, drained

3 tablespoons thin soy sauce

salt

3 tablespoons dry sherry

juice of 1 small orange

Duckling is one of the favourite meats of the Vietnamese and the succulent, moist and rich flavoured duck in this recipe is cunningly combined with the unique flavour of Chinese mushrooms, orange, soy sauce and sherry. I like to serve the portions of duckling in wide soup bowls and hand round chunks of hot crusty bread to mop up the juices. You could equally well serve it with rice, then follow with a crisp green salad.

2 **4** 2 OVEN RANGE, 4 OVEN RANGE, THERMODIAL-CONTROLLED RANGE: Rinse the duckling then place in a large pan of boiling water and simmer uncovered for 15 minutes. Trim the stalks from the mushrooms then slice in half, reserving the soaking liquid. Place the orange rind in a small pan, cover with water, bring to the boil and simmer for 4 minutes. Drain and rinse in cold water.

Drain the duckling then transfer breast-side down into a large flameproof casserole. Half cover with fresh water, add the bamboo shoots, soy sauce, salt to taste, mushrooms and their soaking liquid. Bring to the boil, cover, transfer to the Simmering Plate and simmer gently for 1¼ hours. Remove from the heat and allow to stand for a few minutes, then skim off any fat.

Add the sherry, bring back to the boil and simmer, uncovered, for 20 minutes. Gently lift the duck from the casserole, cut into 4 portions and keep warm.

Add the orange juice and orange rind shreds and most of the spring onion to the casserole. Boil for a further 10 minutes to reduce the liquid.

Return the duckling to the casserole, baste well with the juices and cook for a further 5 minutes. Serve in deep soup plates garnished with the remaining spring onion.

DUCK AND FENNEL CASSEROLE

SERVES 4

2 tablespoons oil

4 duck joints, trimmed of excess fat

12 small shallots, peeled

2 cloves garlic, crushed

4 carrots, cut into bite-size pieces

2 bulbs fennel, cut into bite-size pieces

3 tablespoons wholemeal flour

750 ml (1¼ pint) stock

juice of 1 lemon

3 tablespoons ginger wine or dry sherry

salt and pepper

chopped parsley or fennel, to garnish (optional)

 This is a most flavoursome casserole, ideal to cook ahead. Serve it with a cooked long-grain basmati and wild rice mix.

Heat the oil in a large flameproof casserole, add the duck joints and brown on all sides, about 5 minutes. Remove from the pan with a slotted spoon and set aside.

Add the shallots, garlic, carrots and fennel to the pan juices and cook for 10 minutes, stirring frequently. Stir in the flour then gradually add the stock, blending well. Stir in the lemon juice, wine or sherry and salt and pepper to taste. Bring to the boil, stirring constantly until thickened. Add the duck joints, cover and simmer for 5 minutes.

2 **4** 2 OVEN RANGE AND 4 OVEN RANGE: Transfer to the Simmering Oven and cook for about 1½-2 hours or until the duck is tender.

THERMODIAL-CONTROLLED RANGE: Transfer to the oven set at 160°C/ 325°F and cook for about 1½ hours or until the duck is tender.

Serve hot sprinkled with the chopped parsley or fennel, if you prefer.

PHEASANT CASSEROLE

SERVES 4-6

2 pheasants

4 rashers smoked bacon, rinded and cut in half

2 sticks celery, sliced

12 shallots or baby onions, peeled

2 cloves garlic, crushed

3 sprigs fresh thyme

3 carrots, peeled and chopped

300 ml (½ pint) red wine

3 tablespoons olive oil

2 teaspoons plain flour

150 ml (¼ pint) chicken stock

salt and pepper

2 courgettes, sliced

chopped parsley, to garnish

fried bread shapes, to serve (optional)

 This is a classic dish ideal to make at the end of the game season when birds can tend to be a little old and rather tough – the long cooking and simmering in the range produces a tender and flavoursome meal.

Joint the pheasants into serving size pieces and wrap each piece in a halved rasher of bacon. Secure in place with a wooden cocktail stick. Place in a bowl with the celery, shallots or onions, garlic, thyme, carrots and red wine. Cover and leave to marinate for about 3-4 hours.

Remove the pheasants from the marinade with a slotted spoon. Heat the oil in a large heavy-based flameproof casserole, add the pheasant pieces and brown quickly on all sides until golden. Remove with a slotted spoon and set aside.

Remove the vegetables from the marinade with a slotted spoon and add to the pan juices and quickly fry until golden, about 10 minutes. Sprinkle in the flour then stir in the reserved marinade, stirring constantly. Stir in the stock, return the pheasant to the pan and season with salt and pepper to taste. Bring to the boil and simmer for 5 minutes.

2 **4** 2 OVEN RANGE AND 4 OVEN RANGE: Transfer to the floor of the Simmering Oven and cook for 3 hours. Add the courgettes, mixing well and cook for a further 30 minutes or until the pheasant is tender and the vegetables are cooked.

THERMODIAL-CONTROLLED RANGE: Cook the casserole in the oven set at 150°C/300°F for 2½ hours, add the courgettes, mixing well and cook for a further 30 minutes or until the pheasant is tender and the vegetables are cooked. Alternatively, cook in the Simmering/Warming Oven for 6-8 hours, adding the courgettes for the final 30 minutes cooking time.

Sprinkle with chopped parsley to garnish and serve with fried bread shapes if you like.

VENISON CASSEROLE FROM THE HIGHLANDS

SERVES 6-8

900 g (2 lb) stewing venison

2 tablespoons seasoned flour

4 tablespoons oil

2 onions, cut into wedges

3 sticks celery, sliced

225 g (8 oz) small carrots

100 g (4 oz) streaky bacon, rinded and chopped

450 ml (¾ pint) game or chicken stock

150 ml (¼ pint) red wine

100 g (4 oz) canned chestnuts (optional)

1 bay leaf

6 juniper berries, crushed

½ teaspoon dried thyme

salt and pepper

2 tablespoons blackcurrant or redcurrant jelly

Venison of the farmed type is now readily available and when I drive North to see my family I pass perhaps one of the largest venison farms – in the depths of Yorkshire! Whether your venison is of the wild type and comes from Scotland or of the farmed variety this is one of the very best recipes for cooking the less tender cuts and originates from Scotland.

Cut the venison into bite-size pieces and coat in the seasoned flour. Heat the oil in a large flameproof casserole, add the venison and cook until browned on all sides. Remove from the pan with a slotted spoon and reserve. Add the onions, celery, carrots and bacon to the pan juices and cook until the bacon is crisp and golden. Return the venison to the pan with the stock, wine, chestnuts if used, bay leaf, juniper berries, thyme and salt and pepper to taste. Bring to the boil, transfer to the Simmering Plate and cook for 5 minutes. Stir in the blackcurrant jelly.

2 4 2 OVEN RANGE AND 4 OVEN RANGE: Transfer to the floor of the Simmering Oven and cook for about 4 hours or until the venison is tender.

THERMODIAL-CONTROLLED RANGE: Transfer to the oven set at 160°C/325°F and cook for 2½-3 hours or until the venison is tender. Alternatively, cook in the Simmering/Warming Oven for 6-8 hours or until the venison is tender.

VEGETABLES AND SALADS

VERSATILE VEGETABLES

A whole host of vegetables can be cooked in and on top of the country range and they can be boiled, steamed, baked, fried and sautéed in much the same way as they are prepared using the ordinary electric or gas cooker. When serving a selection of vegetables I like to present them on a huge roomy platter, grouped so that the colours remain strong and the shapes distinctive. They don't have to be terribly special. Simple baby vegetables carefully scrubbed or peeled, boiled then tossed in a little flavoured butter, look stunning when you can admire their shape and form. Even puréed or creamed vegetables look good this way if they are piled into fluffy, billowy mounds then topped with a few browned onion rings or dusted with a few buttered breadcrumbs. I do the same with roast vegetables, often preferring to serve a selection than one huge bowlful of the same and group them on a shallow plate so that you can see roast chunks of potato alongside slim tapering pieces of parsnip and golden roast globes of onions with fat cloves of roast garlic. The same applies to stir-fries and vegetable medleys – all look best in a shallow dish rather than a deep-sided container that hides their appearances.

COOKING GREEN VEGETABLES
IN THE SIMMERING OVEN

Green vegetables needn't just be cooked on top of the range but can be also cooked in the Simmering Oven. Place boiling water to a depth of 2 cm (¾ inch) in the bottom of a saucepan. Add salt to taste and the green vegetables. Bring back to the boil on the Boiling Plate so that the water nearly boils to the top of the pan. Remove from the heat and transfer to the floor of the Simmering Oven and cook for the remaining time until just tender but still crisp.

COOKING DRIED BEANS ON AND IN THE RANGE

Wash the chosen dried beans and place in a pan with water to cover. Cover and bring to the boil and cook for 10 minutes. Remove from the heat then stand the pan on top of the range for 2 hours. Drain and cover with fresh water, adding any seasonings.

2 OVEN RANGE: Bring to the boil then transfer to the floor of the Simmering Oven and cook for 30 minutes. Remove from the oven and leave to stand on top of the range overnight. Drain and use as liked.

 4 OVEN RANGE: Bring to the boil then transfer to the Simmering or Baking Oven and cook for 30 minutes. Remove from the oven and leave to stand on top of the range overnight. Drain and use as liked.

THERMODIAL-CONTROLLED RANGE: Bring to the boil then transfer to the Warming Oven and cook overnight.

COUNTRY RANGE ROASTIES

 Roast potatoes, parsnips and onions make splendid partners to roast meats of all kinds and the country range ensures they arrive to the table crisp and golden without a hint of sogginess!

ROAST POTATOES: Allow about 675 g (1½ lb) old potatoes for 4 people. Peel and cut into even-sized pieces and par-boil in water for about 3-5 minutes. Drain well. Place a little butter and oil in the bottom of a small roasting tin and place on the floor of the Roasting oven or even set at 200-220°C/400-425°F until very hot and sizzling. Add the potatoes and turn on all sides to coat evenly. Cook for about 1¼ hours, turning occasionally until crisp and golden. Drain on absorbent kitchen paper before serving.

ROAST PARSNIPS: Allow about 8 medium parsnips for 4 people. Peel and cut into even-sized pieces or leave whole if preferred. Par-boil in water for about 3-5 minutes. Drain well. Place a little butter and oil in the bottom of a small roasting tin and place on the floor of the Roasting Oven or oven set at 200-220°C/400-425°F until very hot and sizzling. Add the parsnips and turn on all sides to coat evenly. Cook for about 45 minutes, turning occasionally until crisp and golden. Drain on absorbent kitchen paper before serving.

ROAST ONIONS: These are really baked onions and have a wonderfully soft texture after cooking – serve like jacket potatoes, whole with a cross in the top or halved to reveal the flesh. You will need one large onion per person – the bigger hand-sized onions work best. Wash the onions but leave the skins on. Place in a roasting tin and cook near the bottom of the Roasting Oven or oven set at 200-220°C/400-425°F for 1 hour. Transfer to the Simmering or Warming Oven and cook for a further 1-1½ hours until tender.

OPPOSITE:
Oven Baked Peperonata

PLAIN AND DINNER JACKETS

 Jacket potatoes from the country range have unrivalled superiority over their traditional oven and microwave cousins. Potatoes cooked in their skins in the range emerge from the oven with crisp, golden skins yet with fluffy soft centres. Served plain topped with butter or soured cream they are heavenly but when scooped out, mixed with other ingredients, returned to their skins and baked until crisp are irresistible!

PLAIN JACKETS: Scrub one large jacket potato per person, prick with a fork and brush with oil if liked.

2 **4** 2 OVEN RANGE AND 4 OVEN RANGE: Cook near the top of the Roasting Oven for about 1¼ hours.

THERMODIAL-CONTROLLED OVEN: Cook near the top of the oven set at 200-220°C/400-425°F for about 1¼ hours.

Cut in half or make a deep cross in each potato, top with butter or soured cream to serve if you like.

DINNER JACKETS: Cook the potatoes as above, cut in half and scoop out the middles with a spoon leaving a small potato layer inside the skin. Mix with a little milk or butter and the flavourings of your choice. Season to taste, sprinkle with cheese if you like then place on a baking sheet. Return to the oven and cook for a further 15 minutes or until crisp, golden and bubbly.

FILLING IDEAS

- Spicy Sausage – mix the flesh of 1 potato with a little butter, 1 teaspoon snipped chives, a little American mustard, 1 cooked and sliced plain or spiced sausage then top with a little grated cheese.

- Prawn and Spring Onion – mix the flesh of 1 potato with a little butter, 25-50 g (1-2 oz) peeled prawns, 1 finely chopped spring onion, a little grated lemon rind, a little chopped parsley and a pinch of cayenne pepper.

- Bacon and Mushroom – mix the flesh of 1 potato with 1 chopped or crumbled cooked bacon rasher, a little butter, 25 g (1 oz) cooked mushrooms and salt and pepper to taste.

- Cheese and Chive – mix the flesh of 1 potato with 25 g (1 oz) cubed Brie cheese, a little butter, 1 teaspoon snipped chives and salt and pepper to taste.

OPPOSITE:
Wild Rice with Leek and
Toasted Walnuts

SIZZLED CREAMED PARSNIPS

SERVES 4

1 kg (2 lb) parsnips

milk

3 heaped tablespoons natural
low-fat fromage frais

salt and pepper

2 tablespoons walnut oil

2 cloves garlic, thinly sliced

25 g (1 oz) walnuts, coarsely
broken into small pieces

2 tablespoons chopped fresh
parsley

 Older, more mature, parsnips are better served creamed rather than steamed or roasted. The recipe below involves cooking them in milk to preserve the subtle sweet flavour, mashing them to a light purée, then topping them with sizzling garlic and nut oil.

 2 OVEN RANGE, 4 OVEN RANGE, THERMODIAL-CONTROLLED RANGE: Peel the parsnips and cut into 2.5 cm (1 inch) cubes or pieces. Place in a pan and add sufficient milk to barely cover. Bring to the boil on the Boiling Plate, transfer to the Simmering Plate, partially cover and cook for about 15 minutes or until tender.

Drain thoroughly then purée in a blender with the fromage frais and salt and pepper to taste until smooth and fluffy. Alternatively, add the fromage frais and seasoning and beat with an electric hand whisk until smooth and fluffy. Place in a heated serving dish and keep warm.

Place the oil in a small frying pan and heat on the Boiling Plate until hot. Add the garlic and walnuts and cook for 1½-2 minutes. Remove from the heat, stir in the parsley, mixing well then drizzle the sizzling mixture over the top of the creamed parsnips. Serve at once.

POMMES DAUPHINOISE

SERVES 4-6

900 g (2 lb) potatoes

300 ml (½ pint) double cream

4 tablespoons freshly-grated
Parmesan cheese

8 tablespoons grated Gruyère
cheese

salt and pepper

 This classic potato dish is terrific with plain roasts and grills. It is also ideal to make when meal times are somewhat flexible since it will keep warm in the Simmering Oven for a good 30-40 minutes after cooking without spoiling.

Peel the potatoes and cut into thin slices. Place a layer in the base of a 1.8 litre (3 pint) shallow buttered ovenproof dish and spoon over a little of the cream. Sprinkle with some of the Parmesan and Gruyère cheese and season with salt and pepper. Continue to layer in this way finishing with a layer of potatoes that are drizzled with cream. Cover with foil.

2 4 2 OVEN RANGE AND 4 OVEN RANGE: Cook in the Roasting Oven with the grid shelf on the second set of runners for about 45 minutes. Remove the foil and cook for a further 20-25 minutes or until tender and golden on top.

THERMODIAL-CONTROLLED RANGE: Cook in the oven set at 190°C/375°F for about 45 minutes. Remove the foil and cook for a further 30 minutes or until tender and golden on top.

OVEN-BAKED PEPERONATA

SERVES 4

3 tablespoons virgin olive oil

1 onion, chopped

2 cloves garlic, crushed

2 red peppers, cored, seeded and sliced

2 yellow peppers, cored, seeded and sliced

8 ripe tomatoes, peeled, seeded and chopped

pinch of dried herbes de Provence

dash of balsamic vinegar

salt and pepper

 Peppers, onion, garlic and tomatoes are all slow-cooked in this vegetable dish that is perfect with grills and roasts or served at room temperature as a starter with peasant-style crusty bread. The tomatoes should be ripe and flavoursome – look out for the ones that are marked 'grown for flavour'.

Heat the oil in a large heavy-based pan on the Simmering Plate. Add the onion and garlic and cook gently for about 15 minutes until very tender.

Add the peppers and cook for a further 15 minutes, stirring occasionally. Add the tomatoes and herbs and cook for 5 minutes.

2 **4** 2 OVEN RANGE AND 4 OVEN RANGE: Cover and transfer to the Simmering Oven and cook for about 45 minutes or until the peppers and tomatoes are tender and soft and the juices have thickened slightly. Add the vinegar and salt and pepper to taste.

THERMODIAL-CONTROLLED RANGE: Cover and transfer to the oven set at 160°C/325°F for about 35-45 minutes or until the peppers and tomatoes are tender and soft and the juices have thickened slightly. Add the vinegar and salt and pepper to taste.

Allow to cool until warm or at room temperature before serving.

LEMON ZESTED BRUSSELS SPROUTS WITH CHESTNUTS

SERVES 4

225 g (8 oz) fresh chestnuts

salt and pepper

450 g (1 lb) small button Brussels sprouts, trimmed

15 g (½ oz) butter

grated rind of 1 small lemon

 Brussels sprouts have never been my favourite vegetable but cooked with chestnuts in a lemony flavoured butter they are irresistible. If you can't find fresh chestnuts then use whole frozen ones but defrost first.

 2 OVEN RANGE, 4 OVEN RANGE, THERMODIAL-CONTROLLED RANGE: Cook the chestnuts in boiling salted water for 5 minutes. Drain, cool slightly, score the dark skin, peel off and discard. Rub in a clean cloth or teatowel to remove the membrane.

Cook the Brussels sprouts in boiling salted water for about 8-10 minutes until tender, adding the chestnuts for the final 4 minutes cooking time.

Drain thoroughly, return to the pan, add the butter, lemon rind and salt and pepper to taste and toss gently to coat. Transfer to a warmed dish to serve.

HEREFORDSHIRE RED CABBAGE

SERVES 6

1 medium red cabbage

450 g (1 lb) dessert apples, peeled, cored and sliced

150 ml (¼ pint) unsweetened apple juice

1 tablespoon caster sugar

1 teaspoon salt

4 cloves

6 tablespoons red wine vinegar

50 g (2 oz) butter

1 tablespoon redcurrant jelly

salt and pepper

 I simply love this rich and fruity vegetable dish with roast beef and all the trimmings but it is equally as good with a stew, hot pot or with plain grilled meat or sausages. It is also wonderfully temperature tolerant and will keep waiting for what seems like hours or can be reheated very successfully.

Shred the cabbage finely and place in a pan with the apples. Add the apple juice, sugar, salt and cloves. Cover and bring to the boil.

 2 OVEN RANGE AND 4 OVEN RANGE: Transfer to the floor of the Simmering Oven and cook for about 45 minutes.

 THERMODIAL-CONTROLLED RANGE: Transfer to the oven set at 160°C/ 325°F and cook for about 45-50 minutes.

Transfer to the Simmering Plate and remove and discard the cloves. Add the vinegar, butter and redcurrant jelly. Reheat gently and mix well to blend. Season to taste and serve hot.

SPICED COUSCOUS SALAD

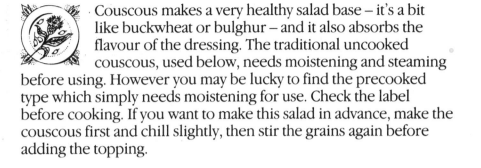

SERVES 6

225 g (8 oz) couscous

1 teaspoon salt

300 ml (½ pint) water

1 lemon

2½ oranges

3 tablespoons olive oil

salt and pepper

¼ cucumber, thinly sliced

4 firm tomatoes, quartered or
6-8 cherry tomatoes

3 eggs, hard-boiled

1 x 50 g (2 oz) can anchovy
fillets, drained

50 g (2 oz) pine nuts, toasted

150 ml (¼ pint) Greek natural
yogurt

2 cloves garlic, crushed

2 teaspoons curry powder

To garnish

fresh coriander sprigs

about 12 stoned black olives

· Couscous makes a very healthy salad base – it's a bit like buckwheat or bulghur – and it also absorbs the flavour of the dressing. The traditional uncooked couscous, used below, needs moistening and steaming before using. However you may be lucky to find the precooked type which simply needs moistening for use. Check the label before cooking. If you want to make this salad in advance, make the couscous first and chill slightly, then stir the grains again before adding the topping.

2 | 4 | 🌡 2 OVEN RANGE, 4 OVEN RANGE, THERMODIAL-CONTROLLED RANGE: Place the couscous in a bowl then stir in the salt and the water. Leave to soak for about 5 minutes until the water is absorbed, then rub the grains between your fingers until smooth and no lumps remain. Pare the rind from the lemon and place 2-3 pieces in a steamer lined with cheesecloth. Add the couscous, cover and steam for 20-25 minutes over simmering water. Remove to a shallow serving bowl and allow to cool slightly.

Mix the juice from ½ orange with the juice from the lemon, the olive oil and salt and pepper to taste. Pour over the still warm couscous and mix gently.

Peel and thinly slice the remaining oranges over a bowl to catch the juice. Arrange the sliced cucumber and oranges neatly on top of the couscous. Arrange the tomatoes in the middle and quartered eggs around the edge topped with half of the anchovy fillets, halved lengthways. Sprinkle with the pine nuts. Chill until required.

Mix the yogurt with the garlic, remaining orange juice, remaining anchovies, mashed to a paste, and the curry powder. Add salt and pepper to taste.

To serve, garnish the couscous salad with fresh coriander sprigs. Serve the spicy sauce and black olives in separate bowls.

NIRVANA SALAD

SERVES 4

16 small salad waxy potatoes
(Pink Fir for example)

6 sprigs fresh mint

8 dwarf sweetcorn

8 dwarf or baby carrots

8 dwarf or baby asparagus
spears

12 small mangetout

4 boneless corn-fed chicken
breasts, skinned

salt and pepper

2 tablespoons oil

about 100 g (4 oz) mixed salad
leaves (lamb's lettuce,
radicchio, endive and
watercress for example)

4 spring onions, chopped

Dressing

3 tablespoons hazelnut oil

3 tablespoons olive oil

1½ tablespoons cider vinegar

3 tablespoons finely chopped
roasted and skinned hazelnuts

2 cloves garlic, crushed

Here is a truly self-indulgent salad using the very best of baby summer vegetables and succulent corn-fed chicken tossed and moistened in a hazelnut dressing. A splendid lunch dish for hot or chilly summer days and stunning if decorated with a few colourful edible flowers.

 2 OVEN RANGE, 4 OVEN RANGE, THERMODIAL-CONTROLLED RANGE: Add the potatoes and mint to a pan of boiling water, cover and simmer for 15-20 minutes or until tender. Meanwhile, add the sweetcorn, baby carrots and asparagus spears to another pan of boiling water, cover and simmer for 3 minutes. Add the mangetout to the sweetcorn pan and cook for a further 2 minutes. Drain the potatoes and vegetable medley and keep warm.

Meanwhile, cut a few slashes in the skin of the chicken breasts and season liberally with salt and pepper. Heat the oil in a frying pan and sauté the chicken breasts for about 5-6 minutes, turning frequently until light golden and cooked but still juicy. Remove from the pan, drain and keep warm.

Mix the cooked and still warm vegetables with the salad leaves and spring onions and place on a serving plate. Slice the chicken breasts thinly and add to the salad. Quickly whisk the oils with the vinegar, hazelnuts and salt and pepper to taste. Pour over the salad and toss lightly to mix. Serve at once.

CHICKEN SALAD WITH A DIFFERENCE

SERVES 4

450 g (1 lb) chicken breast fillets, skinned

2 tablespoons tomato paste

1½ teaspoons ground cumin

1½ teaspoons ground cinnamon

2 teaspoons toasted coriander seeds, lightly crushed

pinch of ground bay leaves

salt and pepper

6 tablespoons olive oil

1 clove garlic, crushed

1 large red pepper, cored, seeded and sliced

175 g (6 oz) mangetout, trimmed

8 canned water chestnuts, sliced

150 g (5 oz) oyster mushrooms, quartered

2 tablespoons white wine vinegar

sprigs fresh coriander, to garnish

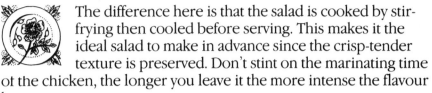 The difference here is that the salad is cooked by stir-frying then cooled before serving. This makes it the ideal salad to make in advance since the crisp-tender texture is preserved. Don't stint on the marinating time of the chicken, the longer you leave it the more intense the flavour becomes.

Cut the chicken breast fillets into thin strips and place in a shallow dish. Mix the tomato paste with the cumin, cinnamon, coriander seeds, ground bay leaves and salt and pepper to taste. Add to the chicken strips and stir well to coat. Cover and leave to stand in a cool place for at least 2 hours.

2 4 🌡 2 OVEN RANGE, 4 OVEN RANGE, THERMODIAL-CONTROLLED RANGE: Heat the oil in a large frying pan or wok, add the garlic, red pepper and mangetout and stir-fry for 2 minutes. Remove with a slotted spoon and reserve.

Add the chicken to the pan juices and stir-fry until cooked and golden, about 3-4 minutes. Add the water chestnuts, mushrooms and wine vinegar and mix well. Remove from the heat and pour the chicken mixture and cooking juices into a large bowl. Add the red pepper and mangetout mixture and toss to mix. Allow to cool then chill until required.

To serve, allow the mixture to come to room temperature then toss well to mix. Serve on individual serving plates, garnished with sprigs of fresh coriander.

RICE, PASTA AND GRAINS

OVEN-COOKED RICE

Rice, in all its guises, can be cooked on the hotplate but can also be cooked successfully in the range oven.

SERVES 4

RICE TYPE	AMOUNT	WATER/STOCK	SALT	COOKING TIME
Basmati	225 g (8 oz)	350 ml (12 fl oz)	½ teaspoon	15-20 mins
Basmati and Wild	225 g (8 oz)	500 ml (17 fl oz)	½ teaspoon	20 mins
Brown	225 g (8 oz)	450 ml (15 fl oz)	½ teaspoon	40-45 mins
Long-grain	225 g (8 oz)	350 ml (12 fl oz)	½ teaspoon	15-20 mins
Thai Fragrant	225 g (8 oz)	450 ml (15 fl oz)	½ teaspoon	10-12 mins

2 **4** 2 OVEN RANGE AND 4 OVEN RANGE: Wash the rice and place in a large flameproof casserole with the water or stock and salt. Bring to the boil, stir well, cover then transfer to the floor of the Simmering Oven and cook for the recommended time. Drain well, rinse if necessary in hot water or fluff with a fork, according to rice type, to serve.

THERMODIAL-CONTROLLED RANGE: Wash the rice and place in a large flameproof casserole with the water or stock and salt. Bring to the boil, stir well, cover then transfer to the oven set at 160°C/325°F and cook for the recommended time. Drain well, rinse if necessary in hot water or fluff with a fork, according to rice type, to serve.

RICE TIPS

- Rice is a very economical cereal, as it increases to about 3 times its original bulk and weight during cooking. For an average appetite, allow about 50 g (2 oz) uncooked rice per serving.

- Rice is fully cooked when it still has a slight bite to it – it should not be totally soft. Fluff rice after cooking by lightly stirring and lifting it with a fork to separate the grains. Stir in a knob of butter if you like.

- Rice will absorb a lot of salt if it is added to the cooking water. If wished, lightly season with sea salt and freshly ground black pepper after cooking.

- Store cooked rice in the refrigerator for up to 2 days. Reheat it only once.

- To reheat cooked rice, place in a pan with 1-2 tablespoons water or stock and heat, stirring over a medium to low heat on the Simmering Plate. Or place the rice and water in a lightly greased casserole, cover and heat in a medium oven until piping hot.

- With some simple additions either before or after cooking, rice is excellent with meat, fish or poultry, served in place of potatoes. Before cooking use flavoured stock instead of water for a change, alternatively use tomato juice or three parts stock plus one part dry white or red wine. For a light-flavoured rice use three-parts vegetable stock plus one part lemon juice and lots of finely grated lemon rind.

- For a rice to serve with grilled steak or hamburgers, fry sliced onions with turmeric and cinnamon. Add rice and beef stock and cook until tender.

- For a rice to serve with roast chicken or curries, fry sliced onions with grated root ginger until tender. Add rice and chicken stock and cook until tender.

- For a rice to serve with boiled bacon, 'grilled' gammon rashers or a poached egg, fry sliced onions and red peppers until tender, add chopped tomatoes and stock and cook until tender.

- For a rice to serve with 'grilled' or baked fish, cook rice in fish or chicken stock then stir in chopped fresh mint, chopped spring onions and diced feta cheese.

- For a rice to serve with curries, cook rice in vegetable stock then stir in chopped coriander and grated lemon rind and juice. Top with toasted cashew nuts.

- For a rice to serve with white meats and fish, cook rice in vegetable stock, lightly fork through a knob of garlic butter and a handful of chopped fresh herbs.

RISOTTO WITH RED WINE AND MUSHROOMS

A well-cooked risotto should be quite moist – in Italy it is often served in a soup bowl with a spoon. Try this richly-flavoured version with steaks, roast beef, venison or grilled sausages.

SERVES 4

1 tablespoon olive oil

1 large onion, thinly sliced

2 teaspoons sugar

2 cloves garlic, crushed

225 g (8 oz) button mushrooms

225 g (8 oz) risotto rice

450 ml (¾ pint) beef or dark vegetable stock

150 ml (¼ pint) dry red wine

pepper

2 4 🌡 2 OVEN RANGE, 4 OVEN RANGE, THERMODIAL-CONTROLLED RANGE: Heat the oil in a frying pan, add the onion and sprinkle over the sugar and cook until tender and golden brown, stirring frequently. Add the garlic, mushrooms and rice and continue to cook for 2-3 minutes, stirring constantly.

Add the stock and wine, bring to the boil, cover, transfer to the Simmering Plate and cook for about 15 minutes or until the rice has absorbed the liquid and is tender. Season to taste with freshly ground black pepper, fluff with a fork and serve at once.

SIMPLE BUT DELICIOUS COUSCOUS

Sometimes the simplest dishes taste the best and this one, simple though it may be, is delicious. The herbs add just enough flavour and interest to stimulate the tastebuds but they don't overpower the delicate flavour and texture of the couscous.

SERVES 4

350 ml (12 fl oz) water

2 tablespoons olive oil

½ teaspoon cumin seeds

½ teaspoon salt

250 g (8 oz) couscous

6 spring onions, thinly sliced

4-5 tablespoons chopped parsley

freshly ground pepper

2 4 🌡 2 OVEN RANGE, 4 OVEN RANGE, THERMODIAL-CONTROLLED RANGE: Place the water, oil, cumin seeds and salt in a large pan and bring the mixture to the boil. Remove from the heat, add the couscous and allow the mixture to stand, covered, for 5 minutes.

Fluff the mixture with a fork and stir in the spring onions, parsley and pepper to taste, mixing well. Serve at once.

MISSISSIPPI RED RICE WITH HAM

SERVES 4

2 tablespoons bacon fat or oil

1 large onion, chopped

3 sticks celery, chopped

1 red pepper, cored, seeded and chopped

450 g (1 lb) cooked ham, cubed

225 g (8 oz) long-grain white rice

1 x 425 g (15 oz) can peeled tomatoes

2 tablespoons tomato purée

1 teaspoon mustard powder

1 teaspoon cayenne pepper

pinch of dried sage

freshly ground black pepper

600 ml (1 pint) light stock

parsley sprigs, to garnish

 A lovely one-pot meal rich with tomatoes and red pepper. The finished dish should have very little liquid showing, but should not be dry.

Heat the bacon fat or oil in a large flameproof casserole, add the onion, celery and pepper and gently sauté until softened, about 5 minutes. Add the ham and cook until it browns slightly. Add the rice and stir-fry until golden. Add the tomatoes and their juice, tomato purée, mustard powder, cayenne pepper, sage, pepper to taste and the stock, mixing well. Bring to the boil, stir well and cover.

 2 OVEN RANGE AND 4 OVEN RANGE: Transfer the casserole to the floor of the Simmering Oven and allow to cook for 15-20 minutes, or until the rice is tender and almost all of the liquid has been absorbed.

THERMODIAL-CONTROLLED RANGE: Transfer the casserole to the oven set at 180°C/350°F and cook for 15-20 minutes or until the rice is tender and almost all of the liquid has been absorbed.

Serve hot, garnished with parsley sprigs.

MIXED MUSHROOM AND COURGETTE RISOTTO

SERVES 4

2 teaspoons olive oil

1 onion, finely chopped

1 clove garlic, crushed

225 g (8 oz) Arborio risotto rice

900 ml (1½ pints) good-quality hot vegetable stock

25 g (1 oz) butter

175 g (6 oz) mixed variety mushrooms (chanterelles, oysters and morels for example or soaked dried porcini mushrooms)

1 courgette, cut into fine julienne strips

450 ml (¾ pint) good-quality chicken stock

1 tablespoon chopped parsley

1 tablespoon chopped fresh basil

3 tablespoons grated Pecorino or Parmesan cheese

salt and pepper

flat-leafed parsley to garnish

In this recipe risotto rice is cooked with stock, onions, garlic, mushrooms and courgettes then flavoured with herbs and grated pecorino cheese. For presentation it is moulded onto a plate, surrounded with more stock and garnished extravagantly with herbs and vegetables. You can use any shape of biscuit cutter for shaping the risotto – heart-shaped and moon-shaped look very attractive. It makes a superb if hearty starter or can be served as a light main course.

2 4 🌡 2 OVEN RANGE, 4 OVEN RANGE, THERMODIAL-CONTROLLED RANGE: Heat the oil in a large heavy-based saucepan, add the onion and garlic and cook gently until softened, about 5 minutes.

Add the rice and cook for 2 minutes, stirring to coat the rice grains with the flavoured onion mixture. Pour in one-quarter of the hot vegetable stock, bring to a gentle boil and stir until absorbed. Gradually stir in the remaining stock, in stages, allowing the liquid to be absorbed before you add more. This should take about 25-30 minutes.

Meanwhile, melt half of the butter in a pan, add the mushrooms and courgettes and cook until softened slightly but still with some bite. Add the chicken stock and cook for 2 minutes. Remove the mushrooms and courgettes from the stock with a slotted spoon and keep warm. Return the stock to the heat and boil until reduced by about half and the mixture is slightly syrupy.

Add the mushrooms and courgettes to the risotto, reserving a few mushrooms to garnish, with the parsley, basil, cheese, remaining butter and salt and pepper to taste. Stir well to mix.

To serve, lay a deep decorative biscuit cutter in the centre of a heated individual serving plate. Spoon the risotto into it, pressing down firmly to pack, then remove the cutter. Repeat with the remaining three portions of risotto. Spoon the reduced stock around each mould and garnish with the reserved mushrooms and flat-leaf parsley. Serve at once.

FETTUCINE WITH DOLCELATTE AND BACON

SERVES 6

225 g (8 oz) smoked streaky bacon, rinds removed

600 ml (1 pint) double cream

450 g (1 lb) Dolcelatte cheese, crumbled

salt and freshly ground black pepper

2 teaspoons olive oil

550 g (1¼ lb) dried fettucine or tagliatelle pasta

2 tablespoons chopped fresh parsley

 This is really fasta pasta since it is so quick and easy to prepare. I like to serve it simply with just a salad accompaniment – a salad leaf and citrus fruit one, like chicory and orange, is ideal since it has a sharp contrasting flavour to the rich creaminess of the pasta dish.

Either place the bacon on a rack in a large roasting tin or place straight into the bottom of the tin.

2 **4** 2 OVEN RANGE AND 4 OVEN RANGE: Either cook the bacon on the rack in the tin in the Roasting Oven with the grid shelf on the highest set of runners for about 6-8 minutes, turning over once, or place the bacon directly in the tin on the floor of the Roasting Oven and cook for 6-8 minutes, turning over once.

THERMODIAL-CONTROLLED RANGE: Either cook the bacon on the rack in the tin in the oven set at 220-230°C/425-450°F with the grid shelf on the highest set of runners for about 6-8 minutes, turning over once, or place the bacon directly in the tin on the floor of the oven and cook for 6-8 minutes, turning over once.

Drain on absorbent kitchen paper and leave to cool then chop or crumble.

Meanwhile, place the cream and cheese in the top of a double boiler over lightly simmering water and cook, stirring frequently until the cheese melts. Add the bacon and pepper to taste. Keep warm while cooking the pasta.

Bring a large pan of salted water to the boil on the Boiling Plate. Add the olive oil and pasta and cook, uncovered, until the pasta is al dente, according to the packet instructions, about 6 minutes. Drain thoroughly and place in a heated serving bowl.

Pour the dolcelatte sauce over the pasta, add half of the parsley and toss gently to mix. Sprinkle with the remaining parsley and serve at once.

PENNE WITH SIZZLED CHORIZO AND CHICKEN LIVERS IN A WALNUT AND HERB SAUCE

SERVES 4

50 g (2 oz) shelled walnuts

1 tablespoon capers

1 tablespoon chopped fresh parsley

1 tablespoon chopped fresh sage

2 tablespoons tarragon vinegar

2 tablespoons olive oil

100 g (4 oz) chorizo sausage, sliced

450 g (1 lb) chicken livers, washed, trimmed and cut into bite-sized pieces

275 g (10 oz) dried penne pasta

freshly ground black pepper

 Penne is the pasta I have chosen for this quickly cooked and tossed main course dish but you can really use any pasta shape. Fresh or dried pasta can be used but be sure to follow the packet instructions so that the pasta is cooked al dente. Serve with a mixed green leaf salad.

2 **4** 🌡 2 OVEN RANGE, 4 OVEN RANGE, THERMODIAL-CONTROLLED RANGE: Place the walnuts, capers, parsley, sage and vinegar in a food processor or blender and process for about 10 seconds to make a grainy sauce.

Heat the oil in a heavy-based frying pan, add the chorizo sausage and fry until browned on all sides, about 5 minutes. Remove from the pan with a slotted spoon and keep warm.

Add the chicken livers to the pan and fry until browned on all sides but the insides are still pink and tender, about 4 minutes. Add the prepared sauce and mix well. Cook over a very gentle heat for a further 4-5 minutes, stirring occasionally.

Meanwhile, cook the pasta in a pan of lightly salted boiling water, according to the packet instructions, about 8-10 minutes or until cooked al dente. Drain well and place in a heated serving bowl.

Add the chorizo sausage and chicken liver mixture to the pasta with freshly ground black pepper and toss gently to mix. Serve at once.

WILD RICE WITH LEEKS AND TOASTED WALNUTS

SERVES 2

25 g (1 oz) walnut halves

25 g (1 oz) butter or margarine

2 small leeks, thinly sliced

1 clove garlic, crushed

100 g (4 oz) wild rice mix

250 ml (8 fl oz) vegetable stock

50 ml (2 fl oz) dry white vermouth

1 large avocado

6 slices Parma ham

25 g (1 oz) freshly-grated Parmesan cheese

 This dish, whilst delicious alone, also tastes good with chicken and fish. Vegetarians may like to replace the ham with a lightly boiled chopped egg.

2 **4** 2 OVEN RANGE, 4 OVEN RANGE, THERMODIAL-CONTROLLED RANGE: Heat a large non-stick frying pan, add the walnuts and cook over a fairly high heat until golden brown, stirring constantly. Remove from the pan and set aside.

Melt the butter or margarine in the pan, stir in the leeks and cook, stirring frequently, until just translucent but not browned. Add the garlic and rice mix and continue to cook, stirring constantly, for a further 2 minutes.

Add the stock and vermouth, bring to the boil, cover, transfer to the Simmering Plate and cook for about 20 minutes or until the rice has absorbed the stock and is tender – adding a little extra hot stock if needed to prevent scorching.

Peel, stone and slice the avocado and arrange on two heated serving plates with the slices of Parma ham. Using a fork, lightly stir the Parmesan into the rice then spoon on to the plates and scatter with the toasted walnuts. Serve at once.

VEGETARIAN DISHES

VEGETARIAN LOAF

SERVES 4

450 g (1 lb) carrots, peeled and sliced

350 g (12 oz) parsnips, peeled and sliced

1 clove garlic, crushed

25 g (1 oz) butter or margarine

100 ml (4 fl oz) vegetable stock or water

3 eggs, beaten

100 g (4 oz) Cheddar cheese, grated

salt and pepper

1 tablespoon chopped fresh parsley

225 g (8 oz) whole baby French beans, trimmed and blanched for 1 minute

This is a tasty vegetable and cheese loaf suitable for serving as part of a vegetarian-style meal. The loaf tin can be lined with non-stick paper so that the loaf is easy to turn out for serving. Do remember to allow the loaf to stand for a good five minutes before serving so that it is easier to slice.

Place the carrots, parsnips, garlic, butter and stock or water in a large pan. Cover and bring to the boil on the Boiling Plate, transfer to the Simmering Plate and cook for about 10-15 minutes until tender, giving the pan a good shake from time to time. Remove from the heat and drain if necessary (although you will find all or most of the liquid should have evaporated). Push the mixture through a sieve or purée in a food processor or blender. Mix with the eggs, cheese, salt and pepper to taste and parsley.

Pour half of the mixture into a well-greased 450 g (1 lb) loaf tin, cover with a neat layer of the French beans, then pour over the remaining carrot mixture. Cover with a sheet of greased foil.

 2 OVEN RANGE AND 4 OVEN RANGE: Place the loaf tin on the grid shelf on the lowest set of runners in the Roasting Oven with the cold shelf above and cook for 30-40 minutes or until the mixture is set.

THERMODIAL-CONTROLLED RANGE: Cook in the oven set at 180°C/350°F for about 35-40 minutes or until the mixture is set.

Allow the loaf to stand in the tin for about 5 minutes before serving. Serve hot.

OPPOSITE:
Tofu, Bok Choy and
Cashew Noodle Toss

RICOTTA AND MUSHROOM PARCELS

SERVES 4

350 g (12 oz) closed cup
mushrooms, very finely
chopped

225 g (8 oz) ricotta cheese

grated rind of 1 lemon

1 bunch watercress, trimmed
and very finely chopped

salt and pepper

12 thin pancakes, made from
300 ml (½ pint) pancake batter

40 g (1½ oz) margarine

Sauce

1 tablespoon oil

1 onion, very finely chopped

100 g (4 oz) closed cup
mushrooms, very finely
chopped

200 ml (7 fl oz) water

225 g (8 oz) tomatoes, peeled
and finely chopped

3 bay leaves

2 tablespoons tomato purée

2 teaspoons cornflour

watercress sprigs, to garnish

 I always have a batch of pancakes in the freezer ready to fill at a moment's notice for a meal since I make a double batch whenever cooking and they prove so useful. The filling below is perfect for a vegetarian meal and only needs a salad accompaniment.

Mix the mushrooms with the ricotta, lemon rind, watercress and salt and pepper to taste, mixing well. Divide the mixture between the pancakes and fold to make neat parcels that enclose the mixture. Place the parcels, seam-side down, in a greased shallow baking dish and dot with the remaining margarine. Cover with foil.

 2 OVEN RANGE: Cook in the Roasting Oven with the grid shelf on the lowest set of runners and with the cold plain shelf above for 25 minutes.

 4 OVEN RANGE: Cook in the Baking Oven with the grid shelf on the third set of runners for 25 minutes.

THERMODIAL-CONTROLLED RANGE: Cook in the oven set at 180°C/350°F for 25 minutes.

Meanwhile, to make the tomato sauce, heat the oil in a pan, add the onion and mushrooms and cook until soft, about 5 minutes. Stir in all but 2 teaspoons of the water, the tomatoes, bay leaves, tomato purée and salt and pepper to taste. Bring to the boil and simmer for 10 minutes. Blend the cornflour with the remaining water, then stir into the sauce. Bring to the boil, stirring constantly, until thickened. Remove and discard the bay leaves.

Pour the sauce over the pancakes to serve. Garnish with sprigs of fresh watercress.

OPPOSITE:
Tarte Au Citron

LIZ'S HOMITY PIE

SERVES 4-6

Pastry

175 g (6 oz) plain flour
75 g (3 oz) margarine
2-3 tablespoons iced water

Filling

350 g (12 oz) new potatoes, scrubbed
3 tablespoons oil
2 onions, chopped
2 cloves garlic, crushed
100 g (4 oz) cheese, grated
1 tablespoon milk
1 tablespoon chopped parsley
salt and pepper

 This is my friend Liz's recipe which she says comes from Pennsylvannia. It is a delicious open pie of potatoes, onion and garlic sprinkled with cheese. I use scrubbed new potatoes but any waxy potato will work well. Meat eaters might like to add a little chopped cooked ham or bacon to the mixture to ring the changes.

To make the pastry, sift the flour into a bowl, add the margarine and rub in with the fingertips until the mixture resembles fine breadcrumbs. Stir in sufficient iced water to make a firm but pliable dough. Roll out on a lightly floured surface and use to line a 20-cm (8-inch) pie plate.

Meanwhile, cook the potatoes in boiling water until tender, about 15-20 minutes. Drain and cut into cubes.

Heat the oil in a large heavy-based pan, add the onions and garlic and sauté until softened, about 5 minutes.

Mix the potatoes with the onion mixture, half of the cheese, the milk, parsley and salt and pepper to taste, mixing well. Spoon into the prepared pie plate and spread evenly. Sprinkle with the remaining cheese.

2 **4** 2 OVEN RANGE AND 4 OVEN RANGE: Bake on the floor of the Roasting Oven for about 25-30 minutes or until the pastry is crisp and golden and the cheese is golden and bubbly.

THERMODIAL-CONTROLLED RANGE: Bake on the floor of the oven set at 220°C/425°F for about 25-30 minutes or until the pastry is crisp and golden and the cheese is golden and bubbly.

VEGETABLE AND LENTIL CASSEROLE

SERVES 4-6

2 tablespoons sunflower or olive oil

3 onions, sliced

2 cloves garlic, crushed

2 large leeks, sliced

450 g (1 lb) baby carrots

2 sticks celery, chopped

175 g (6 oz) baby turnips

75 g (3 oz) baby corn

1 teaspoon cumin seeds

1 teaspoon coriander seeds

2.5 cm (1 inch) piece root ginger, peeled and grated

¼ teaspoon turmeric

2 teaspoons vegetable stock paste

750 ml (1¼ pints) boiling water

175 g (6 oz) split red lentils, rinsed

50 g (2 oz) brown or green lentils, rinsed

4 sun-dried tomatoes, snipped into small pieces

1 teaspoon seed mustard

450 g (1 lb) mixed mushrooms

2 tablespoons chopped fresh coriander

2 tablespoons chopped fresh parsley

The vegetarian's, dieter's or health fiend's delight – a nutritious, high-fibre and low-fat casserole bursting with vegetables, seeds, grains and not least a whole host of vitamins and minerals. The cooking time is somewhat approximate since much will depend upon the maturity of the vegetables you use – tender, tiny vegetables needing less time to cook.

Heat the oil in a very large casserole on the Simmering Plate. Add the onions, garlic and leeks and fry for 5 minutes until softened. Add the carrots, celery, turnips and corn and fry for a further 2 minutes. Add the seeds, ginger, turmeric and vegetable stock paste dissolved in the boiling water. Transfer to the Boiling Plate and bring to the boil. Add the lentils, sun-dried tomatoes and mustard, mixing well. Transfer to the Simmering Plate, cover and cook for 5 minutes.

 2 OVEN RANGE, 4 OVEN RANGE, THERMODIAL-CONTROLLED RANGE: Transfer to the Simmering Oven and cook for 40 minutes. Remove from the oven, stir in the mushrooms, re-cover and cook for a further 20-30 minutes or until the vegetables and lentils are tender.

Taste and adjust the seasoning if necessary. Stir in the coriander and parsley and serve at once.

TOFU, BOK CHOY AND CASHEW NOODLE TOSS

SERVES 3-4

1 x 225 g (8 oz) packet medium egg noodles

2 tablespoons smooth peanut butter

4 tablespoons lime juice

1 tablespoon soft brown sugar

2 tablespoons soy sauce

3 tablespoons sunflower oil

1 tablespoon sesame oil

1 clove garlic, crushed

1 tablespoon toasted sesame seeds

1 bunch spring onions, finely chopped

75 g (3 oz) bok choy cabbage, Chinese leaves or Kai Choy (mustard cabbage) very finely shredded

1 x 227 g (8 oz) can water chestnuts, sliced

175 g (6 oz) fresh beansprouts, washed

2 tablespoons olive oil

1 teaspoon grated root ginger

50 g (2 oz) cashew nuts

220 g (8 oz) packet smoked tofu, cubed

fresh coriander sprigs, to garnish

This Chinese inspired warm salad has a whole host of mixed flavours, textures and colours to excite and stimulate the tastebuds. I think tofu is an under-rated ingredient and if you haven't sampled it before then this is a good way to appreciate its subtle flavour and texture.

 2 OVEN RANGE, 4 OVEN RANGE, THERMODIAL-CONTROLLED RANGE: Bring a large pan of water to the boil on the Boiling Plate, add the noodles and immediately remove from the heat. Leave to stand for 6 minutes by which time the noodles will be perfectly cooked. Alternatively, cook according to the packet instructions.

Meanwhile, beat the peanut butter with the lime juice, sugar, soy sauce, sunflower oil, sesame oil, garlic and sesame seeds to make a smooth dressing.

Drain the noodles thoroughly and turn into a heated bowl. Add the dressing and toss well to coat the noodles. Add the spring onions, bok choy, water chestnuts and beansprouts mixing well. Spoon onto a shallow serving plate.

Heat the olive oil in a frying pan on the Boiling Plate until hot. Add the root ginger and stir-fry for 30 seconds. Add the cashew nuts and tofu cubes and stir-fry until lightly browned on all sides, about 2-3 minutes. Spoon over the salad, garnish with coriander sprigs and serve at once.

HERBED POTATO FOCACCIA

SERVES 6

2½ teaspoons dried yeast

250 ml (8 fl oz) warm water

500 g (1 lb 2 oz) plain flour

550 g (1¼ lb) potatoes, peeled, cooked and mashed

4 tablespoons olive oil

2 cloves garlic, crushed

2 teaspoons chopped fresh rosemary or 1 teaspoon dried

salt and pepper

675 g (1½ lb) small red potatoes

 This is a wonderfully savoury potato and wheat flour bread topped with a flavoursome mixture of sliced potatoes, garlic and rosemary. Ideally it should be eaten on the day it is made either warm or at room temperature.

Sprinkle the yeast over the warm water in a small bowl and leave in a warm place until frothy, about 10 minutes.

Mix 450 g (1 lb) of the flour in a bowl with the mashed potatoes and 1 tablespoon salt until the mixture resembles coarse breadcrumbs. Add the yeast and mix well to form a dough. Turn onto a surface and knead in as much of the remaining flour as necessary until the dough is smooth and elastic and no longer is sticky, about 8 minutes. Return to the bowl, add a little of the oil and turn the ball dough in the oil to coat evenly. Cover with cling film and leave on a surface near to the range to prove until doubled in size, about 1½ hours.

Meanwhile, place the garlic, rosemary and remaining oil in a bowl and mix well. Cover and leave to stand.

Knead the dough for a further 3 minutes then roll out to fit a large greased Swiss roll or shallow baking tin measuring 39 cm x 26.5 cm (15½ x 10½ inches). Cover loosely with oiled cling film and leave on a surface near to the range to prove for a further 45 minutes, or until almost doubled in size.

Scrub and slice the potatoes very thinly and arrange on top of the dough so that the pieces overlap each other. Brush liberally with the garlic mixture to coat. Sprinkle with salt and pepper to taste.

2 **4** 2 OVEN RANGE AND 4 OVEN RANGE: Bake in the Roasting Oven with the grid shelf on the bottom set of runners for about 40-50 minutes, or until golden. Cover with foil if the top starts to brown too much.

THERMODIAL-CONTROLLED RANGE: Bake in the bottom of the oven set at 200°C/400°F for about 40-50 minutes, or until golden. Cover with foil if the top starts to brown too much.

INDIAN-STYLE STUFFED PEPPERS WITH CUCUMBER RAITA TOPPING

SERVES 4

100 g (4 oz) red lentils

50 g (2 oz) butter or margarine

1 onion, chopped

1 clove garlic, crushed

1 cooking apple, peeled, cored and chopped

50 g (2 oz) stoned dates, chopped

1 tablespoon ground coriander

2 teaspoons ground cumin

salt and pepper

4 peppers (red, yellow, orange or green or a mixture)

8 tablespoons natural yogurt

5 cm (2 inch) piece cucumber, grated

fresh coriander sprigs, to garnish

A lovely vegetarian main course or supper dish of peppers stuffed with a spicy mixture of lentils mixed with onion, dates and apple then topped with a dollop of cucumber raita for serving.

Wash the lentils and place in a pan and add enough water to cover the lentils by at least 2.5 cm (1 inch). Bring to the boil, lower the heat, cover and simmer for 6-7 minutes then drain thoroughly.

Melt the butter in a pan, add the onion and garlic and fry until just softened, about 5 minutes. Add the apples and dates and cook, stirring constantly for a further 2-3 minutes. Remove from the heat and stir in the drained lentils, coriander, cumin and salt and pepper to taste. Return to the heat and cook for 1 minute.

Meanwhile, halve the peppers lengthways and remove the cores and seeds. Place in a bowl and cover with boiling water. Leave to stand for 5 minutes to soften then drain thoroughly.

Place the peppers in a roasting tin and fill the cavities with the lentil mixture. Cover tightly with foil.

2 4 2 OVEN RANGE AND 4 OVEN RANGE: Cook in the Roasting Oven with the grid shelf on the lowest set of runners for about 30-40 minutes, or until the peppers are tender.

 THERMODIAL-CONTROLLED RANGE: Cook in the oven set at 190°C/ 375°F for about 30-40 minutes, or until the peppers are tender.

Meanwhile, mix the yogurt with the grated cucumber and salt and pepper to taste.

Serve the peppers hot, each topped with a spoonful of the cucumber raita and garnished with a sprig of fresh coriander.

PUDDINGS AND DESSERTS

BRANDIED BREAD AND BUTTER PUDDING

SERVES 6

6 thick slices white bread

40 g (1½ oz) butter, melted

100 g (4 oz) mixed dried fruit (sultanas, currants and no-need-to-soak dried apricots, for example)

grated rind of 1 lemon

50 g (2 oz) caster sugar

2 eggs

2 tablespoons brandy

450 ml (¾ pint) milk

1 tablespoon demerara sugar

1 teaspoon ground cinnamon

I haven't met anyone who doesn't like the nursery favourite Bread and Butter Pudding and this one is doubly delicious with its generous splash or two of brandy. The dried fruit can be varied according to what is in the storecupboard but remember if you use dried apricots they should be of the no-need-to-soak variety.

Remove the crusts from the bread and cut into triangles. Dip in the melted butter on one side and arrange about half of the slices, buttered-sides down in a well greased shallow ovenproof dish (measuring about 18 x 23 cm (7 x 9 inches). Scatter over the dried fruit, lemon rind and half of the caster sugar. Cover with the remaining bread slices.

Beat the eggs with the brandy, milk and remaining sugar and pour over the bread slices. Leave to stand for about 30 minutes then gently push the bread down into the custard to ensure each piece is thoroughly moistened. Sprinkle with the demerara sugar and cinnamon.

2 **4** 2 OVEN RANGE AND 4 OVEN RANGE: Cook in the Roasting Oven with the grid shelf on the floor of the oven for about 25 minutes or until the custard is lightly set and its top golden brown and crispy.

THERMODIAL-CONTROLLED RANGE: Cook in the oven set at 180°C/ 350°F for about 30-35 minutes or until the custard is lightly set and the top is golden brown and crispy.

BROWN BREAD AND HAZELNUT ICE CREAM

SERVES 4

75 g (3 oz) wholemeal breadcrumbs

150 g (5 oz) light muscovado sugar

50 g (2 oz) hazelnuts, chopped

3 egg whites

300 ml (½ pint) double cream

fresh berry fruits and mint or edible flowers, to decorate

A splendid ice cream, easy to make and wonderfully versatile as an emergency freezer pudding. I like to serve it with a mixed array of summer berry fruits like raspberries, loganberries, redcurrants and strawberries and decorated with mint or other edible flowers and their leaves. Needless to say if you want a less rich ice cream then substitute up to half of the cream with natural or hazelnut yogurt.

Mix the breadcrumbs with 50 g (2 oz) of the sugar and the hazelnuts and sprinkle onto a baking sheet.

2 OVEN RANGE AND 4 OVEN RANGE: Place the sheet on the grid shelf on the Roasting Oven floor and cook for 10-15 minutes or until crisp and golden, stirring occasionally so that the mixture browns evenly. Allow to cool.

THERMODIAL-CONTROLLED RANGE: Place the sheet in the oven set at 180°C/350°F and cook for 10-15 minutes or until crisp and golden, stirring occasionally so that the mixture browns evenly. Allow to cool.

Whisk the egg whites until stiff and gently stir in the remaining sugar. Whip the cream until stiff and fold into the egg white mixture using a metal spoon. Fold in the toasted bread, sugar and nut mixture, mixing well. Pour into a freezer-proof container and freeze until firm, at least 2 hours.

Remove from the freezer about 15 minutes before serving to soften slightly. Serve scooped into glasses or onto plates with berries and decorated with mint leaves or edible flowers.

SUMMER ORANGE CUSTARDS WITH CHOCOLATE SAUCE

SERVES 4

1 orange

450 ml (¾ pint) milk

150 ml (¼ pint) crème fraîche or thick cream

few drops of vanilla essence

75 g (3 oz) golden granulated sugar

2 eggs

2 egg yolks

Sauce

175 g (6 oz) good-quality plain dessert chocolate

25 g (1 oz) unsalted butter

150 ml (¼ pint) single cream

icing sugar, to dust

 Make these easy, and always popular, creamy, orange-flavoured custards the day before they are required so they have plenty of time to set. This will ensure that they turn out perfectly, ready to serve with a contrasting and scrumptious chocolate sauce.

Pare a large piece of orange rind from the orange and cut into fine julienne shreds. Place in a cup, cover with boiling water and leave to stand until required. Finely grate the zest from the remaining orange and squeeze and reserve the juice.

Place the milk, crème fraîche, grated orange zest, vanilla and sugar in a pan and bring almost to the boil. Remove from the heat and allow to cool slightly.

Whisk the eggs and egg yolks together and then thoroughly whisk in the hot milk mixture. Strain into 4 large ramekin dishes and place in a roasting tin. Pour in boiling water to come halfway up the sides of the ramekins.

2 **4** 2 OVEN RANGE AND 4 OVEN RANGE: Cook on the lowest set of runners in the Roasting Oven for 10 minutes then transfer to the Simmering Oven floor on a grid shelf and cook for about 30-40 minutes or until just set.

THERMODIAL-CONTROLLED RANGE: Cook in the oven set at 180°C/ 350°F for 40-45 minutes or until just set.

Remove from the roasting tin, allow to cool then chill until firm and set, at least 8 hours.

To make the sauce, break the chocolate into pieces into a small pan, add the butter and heat very gently on the Simmering Plate until melted. Gradually blend in the reserved orange juice and single cream until smooth. Cool then chill.

When ready to serve, loosen the edges of the custard with a knife and turn out onto small serving plates. Dredge with icing sugar and top with the well drained fine shreds of orange rind. Spoon a little chocolate sauce around each chilled custard to serve.

BROWN SUGAR PAVLOVA WITH HOT LEMON SAUCE

SERVES 6

3 egg whites

175 g (6 oz) soft light brown sugar

1 teaspoon cornflour

1 teaspoon lemon juice or vinegar

Filling

300 ml (½ pint) double or whipping cream

450 g (1 lb) prepared mixed fresh fruits

Sauce

finely grated rind and juice of 2 large lemons

50 g (2 oz) butter

50 g (2 oz) caster sugar

150 ml (¼ pint) water

1 tablespoon cornflour

Here is a superb pavlova recipe all the better for filling with whipped cream and a mound of prepared seasonal fruit. In early summer I like to top my pavlova with early English strawberries, a sprinkling of red and blackcurrants and pairs of washed cherries still with stalks on. As the soft fruit season progresses I include raspberries, loganberries, peaches and nectarines finally culminating in a specatcular array of imported exotic fruits like kiwi, passionfruit, mango and papaya. If you prefer a white sugar meringue then use caster sugar instead of the brown sugar.

Mark a 20-cm (8-inch) circle on a sheet of silicone paper on a baking sheet.

Whisk the egg whites until they stand in stiff peaks. Whisk in half of the sugar, a teaspoonful at a time, whisking well until the meringue is thick and glossy. Sift the remaining sugar with the cornflour and whisk into the meringue mixture a little at a time with the lemon juice or vinegar.

Spoon or pipe the meringue on to the silicone paper, following the line of the circle and covering the base but making a hollow in the centre of the meringue to hold the fruit and cream later.

2 **4** 2 OVEN RANGE AND 4 OVEN RANGE: Bake in the Simmering Oven with the grid shelf on the oven floor for 1½ hours. Remove the pavlova from the oven, cover with a second sheet of silicone paper and a wire cooling rack and carefully invert the pavlova onto it so that the base of the pavlova is uppermost. Return to the oven and cook for a further 30-45 minutes or until the base of the pavlova is dry and the silicone paper can be easily removed.

THERMODIAL-CONTROLLED RANGE: Bake in the base of the oven when the range is at idling heat and leave until set and fairly firm. Transfer to the Simmering/Warming Oven to finish the drying process. Total cooking time will be about 2−2¼ hours.

Allow to cool upside down then invert onto a serving plate.

For the filling, whip the cream until it stands in soft peaks. Pile into the centre of the pavlova and top with the prepared fruits.

To make the sauce, place the lemon rind, lemon juice, butter, sugar and water in a pan. Slowly bring to the boil, stirring to dissolve the sugar. Mix the cornflour with a little extra water and stir into the lemon mixture. Return to the boil, stirring constantly, and cook for 2-3 minutes.

Serve the pavlova, cut into wedges, with a little of the hot sauce poured over.

KISSEL FRUIT COMPOTE

SERVES 8

450 g (1 lb) assorted mixed dried fruit (peaches, apricots, apples, pears and prunes, for example)

450 ml (¾ pint) water

100 g (4 oz) cranberries

1 large eating apple, peeled, cored and sliced

1 large cinnamon stick

4 cloves

1 lemon, sliced

175 g (6 oz) fresh cherries, stoned, stalks intact and thoroughly washed

50-100 g (2-4 oz) sugar, to taste

75 g (3 oz) seedless green grapes

4 ripe figs, quartered

grated rind and juice of 1 orange

3 tablespoons cherry brandy

This spiced fruit compote, packed with dried and winter imported fruits like cranberries, figs and grapes, makes a wonderful dessert to crown a festive-style meal. A handful of imported cherries, expensive as they are, give the compote a real touch of luxury.

2 4 🌡 2 OVEN RANGE, 4 OVEN RANGE, THERMODIAL-CONTROLLED RANGE: Place the dried fruit in a pan with the water. Bring to the boil on the Boiling Plate. Transfer to the Simmering Plate, cover and cook gently until tender, about 25 minutes.

Add the cranberries, apple, cinnamon stick, cloves, lemon, cherries and sugar to taste, mixing well. Cover and cook gently for a further 5 minutes or until the flavours are blended but the fruit is still whole and intact.

Remove from the heat, add the grapes, figs, orange rind and juice and brandy. Cover and leave to stand for at least 30 minutes or until required.

Remove and discard the cinnamon stick and transfer to a serving bowl. Serve warm or cold with cream or yogurt.

ITALIAN PANNA COTTA WITH RASPBERRY COULIS

SERVES 6

600 ml (1 pint) double cream

150 g (5 oz) caster sugar

½ vanilla pod or a few drops of real vanilla essence

pared rind of 1 lemon

15 g (½ oz) powdered gelatine

3 tablespoons water

2-3 tablespoons Amaretto liqueur

Raspberry Coulis

225 g (8 oz) raspberries, hulled

25-50 g (1-2 oz) caster sugar

juice of 1 lemon

50 ml (2 fl oz) water

mint sprigs, to decorate

The contrast between the silky smooth texture and delicate taste of this moulded dessert and its rich, vibrant, fruity-flavoured sauce is sharp and delights the tastebuds. Other fruit coulis could be made to ring the changes but make sure they are reasonably sharp and fruity for best effect.

| 2 | 4 | 🌡 |

2 OVEN RANGE, 4 OVEN RANGE, THERMODIAL-CONTROLLED RANGE: Place the cream in a heavy-based saucepan with the sugar, vanilla and lemon rind. Bring slowly to boiling point, stirring well to dissolve the sugar. Remove from the heat, remove the vanilla pod, if using, and lemon rind.

Meanwhile, sprinkle the gelatine over the water in a small bowl and leave until spongy. Place in a pan of hot water and stir until clear and dissolved. Stir into the cream mixture with the Amaretto liqueur to taste, mixing well. Pour into a round or loaf-shaped 900-ml (1½-pint) capacity mould and chill to set, about 4-6 hours.

To make the sauce, place the raspberries, sugar, lemon juice and water in a small pan and bring to the boil, stirring well to dissolve the sugar. Cook for 2 minutes, remove from the heat and leave to cool.

When cool, pass the raspberry mixture through a fine nylon sieve to remove the pips and chill until required.

To serve, dip the mould briefly into hot water to loosen then invert onto a serving dish. Cut into thick slices or wedges to serve with a little of the raspberry coulis. Decorate each portion with a sprig of mint to serve.

BUCKS FIZZ SORBET

SERVES 4

175 g (6 oz) caster sugar

175 ml (6 fl oz) water

250 ml (8 fl oz) chilled Champagne or sparkling wine

2 tablespoons fresh orange juice

¼ teaspoon orange flower water

1 large egg white (size 1)

 I first tasted this sorbet at the beautiful home of Pol Roger in Epernay. Pol Roger champagne is renowned the world over and was the favourite champagne of Winston Churchill. The walls of the château were lined with witty cartoons of Winston (always with glass or bottle of Pol Roger in hand) and maybe it was the champagne but I thought them all hilarious. I didn't have to be pressed to sample this wonderful sorbet – a frozen buck's fizz – but I rarely use Pol Roger champagne when making it at home (much better drunk liquid and bubbly from a glass). The recipe works just as well with a good sparkling wine.

2 **4** 🌡 2 OVEN RANGE, 4 OVEN RANGE, THERMODIAL-CONTROLLED RANGE: Place the sugar and water in a heavy-based pan. Cook, over a gentle heat on the Simmering Plate, until the sugar dissolves, stirring continuously. Bring to the boil, reduce the heat and simmer for 10 minutes. Remove from the heat, allow to cool then chill for 2 hours.

Mix the chilled syrup with the Champagne, orange juice and orange flower water. Pour into a 600-ml (1-pint) rigid freezer-proof container and freeze until half frozen.

Whisk the egg white until it stands in stiff peaks. Whisk the half-frozen water ice until smooth then fold in the egg white with a metal spoon. Return to the freezer-proof container and freeze until firm, about 2-3 hours.

Scoop the sorbet into chilled glasses to serve.

CHOCOLATE MOUSSE ICE CREAM

SERVES 6

100 ml (3½ fl oz) milk

75 g (3 oz) caster sugar

225 g (8 oz) plain dessert chocolate, broken into pieces

450 ml (¾ pint) double cream

3 large egg yolks (size 1 or 2)

 Here is a chocoholics dream come true – possibly the richest chocolate ice cream I have ever tasted. Serve in chilled glasses whose rims have been frosted with sugar and powdered chocolate.

2 **4** 🌡 2 OVEN RANGE, 4 OVEN RANGE, THERMODIAL-CONTROLLED RANGE: Place the milk and sugar in a heavy-based pan and bring to the boil, stirring constantly. Remove from the heat, add the chocolate and stir until the mixture is smooth. Allow to cool.

Whip the cream with the egg yolks and stir into the cooled chocolate mixture. Pour into a rigid freezer container and freeze until half-frozen, about 1-2 hours. Remove from the freezer and whisk until smooth and free from large ice crystals. Return to the freezer and freeze until firm, about 2-4 hours.

Serve scooped into chilled glasses.

MOCHA ROULADE

SERVES 6-8

Roulade

175 g (6 oz) plain chocolate
3 tablespoons water
1 tablespoon instant coffee powder
5 eggs, separated
225 g (8 oz) caster sugar
icing sugar, to dust

Filling

1 tablespoon instant coffee powder
1 tablespoon boiling water
150 ml (¼ pint) double cream
150 ml (¼ pint) fromage frais
1 tablespoon icing sugar
whipped cream and chocolate coated coffee beans, to decorate (optional)

Chocolate roulade has long been a favourite but this coffee and chocolate version upstages it. Decorate with swirls of cream and chocolate-coated coffee beans with extra pouring cream if the waistline will allow.

To make the roulade, break the chocolate into a pan and add the water and coffee powder. Heat gently until the chocolate has melted. Remove from the heat.

Whisk the egg yolks with the sugar until very thick and creamy, then fold in the warm chocolate mixture. Whisk the egg whites until they stand in stiff peaks and fold into the chocolate mixture with a metal spoon. Turn into a greased and lined 20 x 30 cm (8 x 12 inch) Swiss roll tin.

2 2 OVEN RANGE: Cook in the Roasting Oven with the grid shelf on the lowest set of runners and the cold metal shelf above for about 20-25 minutes, or until firm.

4 4 OVEN RANGE: Cook in the Baking Oven with the grid shelf positioned just above the centre of the oven for about 20-25 minutes, or until firm.

 THERMODIAL-CONTROLLED RANGE: Cook in the oven set at 180°C/350°F for about 20-25 minutes, or until firm.

Remove from the oven and leave in the tin for 5 minutes. Cover immediately with a clean damp cloth and leave in the refrigerator overnight.

To serve, carefully remove the cloth and turn the roulade out onto a sheet dusted thickly with icing sugar. Peel away and discard the lining paper. To make the filling, dissolve the coffee in the boiling water. Whip the cream until it stands in soft peaks. Fold in the coffee mixture, fromage frais and icing sugar. Spread over the roulade then roll up to enclose like a Swiss roll. Pipe swirls of cream down the length of the roulade and decorate with chocolate-coated coffee beans if you like. Serve lightly chilled.

TIPSY WHITE PEACH, ORANGE AND WINE JELLY

SERVES 6-8

about 350 ml (12 fl oz) freshly-squeezed orange juice

2 x 11 g (½ oz) sachets powdered gelatine

250 ml (8 fl oz) sweet white wine

2 small oranges, peeled, pith removed and sliced

2 large ripe white peaches, skinned, stoned and sliced

mint leaves, orange slices or segments and white peach slices, to decorate

 This is a jelly for grown-ups that should be set in the most decorative mould you can find. Serve it well chilled with macaroons or shortbread.

2 **4** 🌡 2 OVEN RANGE, 4 OVEN RANGE, THERMODIAL-CONTROLLED RANGE: Place about 4-5 tablespoons of the orange juice in a bowl and sprinkle over the gelatine. Leave until spongy then place the bowl in a pan of hot water to heat and dissolve. Remove from the heat and add the wine and sufficient orange juice to make up to 600 ml (1 pint). Chill until just beginning to set.

When the jelly is just beginning to set, layer the fruit and jelly in a 750 ml (1¼ pint) wetted mould and chill to set, about 2-4 hours.

To serve, dip briefly in very hot water or place a very hot cloth around the mould then invert carefully onto a chilled serving plate. Decorate with mint leaves, orange slices or segments and a few extra slices of white peach. Serve chilled with macaroons or shortbread.

BACCHANALIAN RED FRUITS

SERVES 4-6

25 g (1 oz) caster sugar

150 ml (¼ pint) apple juice

1 teaspoon pink peppercorns, crushed

150 ml (¼ pint) sweet dessert wine

450 g (1 lb) mixed red fruits (strawberries, raspberries and redcurrants, for example)

mint leaves, lemon balm or edible flowers to decorate

 This is a drunken revelry of red summer fruits in a rich wine syrup that is spiked with crushed pink peppercorns. Ideally use a good sweet dessert wine like Beaumes de Venise for the syrup.

2 **4** 🌡 2 OVEN RANGE, 4 OVEN RANGE, THERMODIAL-CONTROLLED RANGE: Place the sugar, apple juice and pink peppercorns in a heavy-based pan and bring gently to the boil on the Simmering Plate. Boil gently for about 5 minutes or until the mixture thickens slightly and becomes syrupy. Remove from the heat, add the wine and leave to cool.

Prepare the fruit according to type and add to the cooled syrup. Cover and leave to soak for at least 30 minutes but not longer than 1 hour before serving.

Spoon into a chilled serving bowl and decorate with sprigs of fresh mint, lemon balm or edible flowers.

NURSERY RICE PUDDING

SERVES 4

50 g (2 oz) round-grain or pudding rice
600 ml (1 pint) milk
1 vanilla pod
1 cinnamon stick
finely grated zest of 1 lemon
25 g (1 oz) caster sugar
15 g (½ oz) butter or margarine
grated nutmeg

 With the welcome return to honest, genuine food many nursery favourites have come to the culinary foreground. Rice pudding is one of these and with a hint of spice, an overtone of zesty lemon, and a wonderfully creamy texture it is much too good for just the children to enjoy. You can add 50 g (2 oz) raisins or other chopped dried fruit to the cooked pudding and heat for a further 5 minutes.

Wash the rice and drain well. Place in an ovenproof dish with the milk, vanilla pod, cinnamon stick, lemon zest, sugar and butter or margarine, mixing well.

2 2 OVEN RANGE: Place in the Roasting Oven with the grid shelf on the lowest set of runners and cook for 25 minutes or until a pale brown skin forms on the pudding. Stir well, sprinkle with grated nutmeg then transfer to the Simmering Oven and cook for a further 1½-2 hours until cooked.

4 4 OVEN RANGE: Cook near the top of the Baking Oven for about 25 minutes or until a pale golden skin forms on the pudding. Stir well, sprinkle with grated nutmeg then transfer to the Simmering Oven and cook for a further 1½-2 hours until cooked.

THERMODIAL-CONTROLLED RANGE: Place near the bottom of the oven set at 140-150°C/275-300°F for at least 2 hours, stirring occasionally.

Remove the vanilla pod and cinnamon stick before serving.

BANOFFI PIE

SERVES 6-8

275 g (10 oz) butter
250 g (9 oz) ginger biscuits, crushed
150 g (5 oz) caster sugar
1 x 397 g (14 oz) can sweetened condensed milk
2 bananas, sliced
1 tablespoon lemon juice
300 ml (½ pint) double cream
chocolate curls, to decorate

 Banoffi pie must rate as one of the all-time favourite desserts with its marvellous combination of sticky toffee and bananas. Serve chilled, or for a softer toffee texture at room temperature.

2 **4** 2 OVEN RANGE, 4 OVEN RANGE, THERMODIAL-CONTROLLED RANGE: Melt 100 g (4 oz) of the butter in a pan over a gentle heat. Stir in the crushed ginger biscuits and mix well. Press onto the base and sides of a 19 cm (7½ inch) loose-bottomed fluted flan tin and chill until firm, about 15 minutes.

Place the remaining butter and sugar in a non-stick pan and heat gently, stirring constantly until the butter melts. Add the condensed milk and heat, stirring constantly until simmering. Simmer on a low boil for exactly 5 minutes to make a light golden caramel. Pour over the prepared biscuit base, allow to cool slightly then chill in the refrigerator.

To serve, toss the bananas in the lemon juice to prevent them turning brown. Whip the cream until it stands in soft peaks. Place a layer of bananas over the toffee layer in the flan. Spread or pipe with the whipped cream. Decorate with the remaining bananas and chocolate curls.

OPPOSITE:
My Italian Flowerpot Loaf

TARTE AU CITRON

Pastry

200 g (7 oz) plain flour

pinch of salt

90 g (3½ oz) butter

60 g (2½ oz) caster sugar

3 egg yolks

¾ teaspoon vanilla essence

Filling

3 eggs

160 g (5½ oz) sugar

grated rind and juice of 2 lemons

160 g (5½ oz) butter, melted

90 g (3½ oz) ground almonds

icing sugar, to dust

julienne strips of lemon zest or thin lemon slices, to decorate (optional)

This has to be one of my all-time favourite desserts . It is super just sprinkled with a dusting of icing sugar but also looks good strewn with candied or plain lemon zest julienne or decorated with very thin slices of lemon.

Sift the flour and salt onto a marble slab or cool surface and make a large well in the centre. Put the butter, sugar, egg yolks and vanilla in the centre and work in with the fingertips, gradually drawing in the flour until the mixture is smooth. Knead lightly then wrap and chill for 30 minutes.

Roll out the pastry on a lightly floured surface and use to line a 25-cm (10-inch) tart tin or flan ring set on a baking sheet, line with greaseproof paper and fill with baking beans.

2 **4** 2 OVEN RANGE AND 4 OVEN RANGE: Cook the pastry case in the Roasting Oven with the grid shelf on the bottom set of runners for 15 minutes.

 THERMODIAL-CONTROLLED RANGE: Cook in the oven set at 190°C/375°F for 15 minutes.

Remove the baking beans and greaseproof paper.

Meanwhile, to make the filling, whisk the eggs and sugar until they are very thick and will leave a trail in the mixture when the beaters are lifted. Stir in the lemon juice and rind then the melted butter and almonds. Pour into the pre-cooked pastry case.

2 2 OVEN RANGE: Cook in the Roasting Oven with the grid shelf on the lowest set of runners and the cold plain shelf above for about 25-30 minutes or until the filling is golden and set.

4 4 OVEN RANGE: Cook near the top of the Baking Oven for about 25-30 minutes or until the filling is golden and set.

THERMODIAL-CONTROLLED OVEN: Reduce the oven temperature to 180°C/350°F and cook for about 25-30 minutes or until the filling is golden and set.

Allow to cool before dusting with icing sugar to serve. Decorate with julienne strips of lemon rind or lemon slices if liked.

VARIATION
ORANGE AND GRAND MARNIER TARTE: Prepare and cook as above but use the grated rind and juice of 1½ oranges instead of the lemons and add 1½ teaspoons Grand Marnier to the filling.

OPPOSITE:
Country Range Preserves, Special Gifts and Dried Flowers

RHUBARB AND GINGER PIE

SERVES 6-8

Pastry

275 g (10 oz) plain flour

pinch of salt

60 g (2½ oz) lard

60 g (2½ oz) butter or margarine

3-4 tablespoons cold water

Filling

900 g (2 lb) rhubarb, sliced

100 g (4 oz) soft light brown sugar

2 tablespoons cornflour

15 g (½ oz) preserved ginger, chopped

milk or beaten egg, to glaze

caster sugar or crushed sugar cubes, to sprinkle

 This is a recipe for a double-crust pie bulging with rhubarb and preserved ginger and all the better for serving with cream, custard, yogurt, ice cream or crème fraîche. If you wish to make an American one-crust pie, made more familiar and certainly enticing by Delia Smith in her television series on Summer Eating and summer recipe collection book, then you will only need 175 g (6 oz) quantities of shortcrust pastry. Roll out on a greased baking sheet to a 25-cm (10-inch) circle, brush with egg yolk, fill with the fruit selection tossed with the sugar and cornflour then gather the pastry around the fruit in a raggy way so that it surrounds the fruit to make a case but does not completely enclose it. Glaze and sprinkle with sugar and bake as below.

Lightly grease the base and sides of a 25-cm (10-inch) pie dish. Prepare the pastry by mixing the flour with the salt. Rub in the lard and butter or margarine until the mixture resembles fine breadcrumbs. Add the water and mix to a firm dough. Roll out two-thirds of the pastry on a lightly floured surface, to a circle large enough to line the base and sides of the dish. Ease the pastry into the dish and trim away the excess. Roll out the remaining pastry and trimmings to make a lid for the pie.

For the filling, place half of the rhubarb in the pie dish. Mix the sugar and cornflour together and sprinkle half of this mixture over the fruit. Sprinkle with the ginger and top with the remaining fruit and cornflour mixture. Brush the rim of the dish with milk or beaten egg and top with the pastry lid. Trim away any excess pastry and seal the edges. Flute the pastry rim attractively and place a small hole in the top of the pie for the steam to escape during cooking (a pie funnel may be placed in the centre of the pie to hold up the crust during cooking). Glaze the pie with milk or beaten egg and sprinkle with the sugar. Decorate the pie top with any pastry trimmings in the shape of leaves or fruit if you like.

2 **4** 2 OVEN RANGE AND 4 OVEN RANGE: Bake on the floor of the Roasting Oven for about 20-25 minutes or until the pastry is a rich golden colour. Transfer to the top of the Simmering Oven and cook for a further 20 minutes.

THERMODIAL-CONTROLLED RANGE: Bake in the oven set at 220°C/ 425°F for about 30-40 minutes or until the pastry is cooked golden brown and the fruit is cooked through. Cover with foil if the top seems to be browning too much.

Serve hot or cold with cream, yogurt, ice cream or crème fraîche.

VARIATIONS

APPLE AND BLACKBERRY PIE: Follow the recipe above but use 450 g (1 lb) hulled blackberries and 450 g (1 lb) sliced apples instead of the rhubarb and ginger.

PLUM AND ORANGE PIE: Follow the recipe above but use 900 g (2 lb) halved and stoned plums with the grated rind of 1 orange instead of the rhubarb and ginger.

GOOSEBERRY, GINGER AND ORANGE: Follow the recipe above but use 900 g (2 lb) topped and tailed gooseberries with the grated rind of 1 orange instead of the rhubarb.

TIRAMISU

SERVES 4

16 sponge fingers

60 ml (2½ fl oz) rum

2 tablespoons brandy or Marsala

90 ml (3½ fl oz) strong, cold black coffee

8-10 small macaroon biscuits

3 tablespoons apricot jam

400 g (14 oz) Mascarpone or other soft cream cheese

2 eggs, separated

4 tablespoons icing sugar

100 g (4 oz) powdered or very finely grated chocolate

 This dessert which roughly translates as 'pick me up' is the Italian's answer to the British trifle. Sponge fingers rather than trifle sponges are layered with soft cream cheese instead of custard and laced with Marsala or brandy instead of sherry. The result is quite beguiling – make double quantities as everyone always asks for second helpings!

Place the sponge fingers on a baking tray.

2 4 2 OVEN RANGE AND 4 OVEN RANGE: Place the sponge fingers in the Roasting Oven with the grid shelf on the first set of runners and bake for 10-15 minutes or until very crisp and dry.

THERMODIAL-CONTROLLED RANGE: Place the sponge fingers in the oven set at 190°C/375°F and cook for 10-15 minutes or until very crisp and dry.

Mix half of the rum with the brandy or Marsala and coffee. Dip the sponge fingers into this mixture so that they soak up a little of the liquid but do not go completely soggy and place in the bottom of a shallow serving dish.

Spread the macaroon biscuits with the jam and arrange over the sponge fingers. Sprinkle over any remaining coffee mixture.

Mix the cream cheese with the egg yolks, icing sugar and remaining rum. Whisk the egg whites until they stand in stiff peaks, then fold into the cheese mixture with a metal spoon. Spoon over the macaroons to cover completely. Sprinkle with a thick layer of the chocolate, cover and chill overnight or for at least 6 hours before serving.

HOME BAKING

OUR DAILY BREAD

Makes 2 x 450 g (1 lb) loaves,
1 x 900 g (2 lb) loaf or 12 rolls

---

675 g (1½ lb) strong white or
wholemeal flour or half/half
mixture of both

---

2 teaspoons salt

---

25 g (1 oz) butter or margarine

---

20 g (¾ oz) fresh yeast (or the
equivalent recommended
dried yeast – see
manufacturer's packet
instructions)

---

450 ml (¾ pint) hand hot water

Optional

---

beaten egg, to glaze

---

poppy seeds, sesame seeds,
rolled oats, cumin seeds,
caraway seeds or nibbed
wheat, to sprinkle

 Whilst testing the recipes for this book I have re-discovered the joys of breadmaking. The stress-relieving antics of bashing a piece of dough; sitting back and watching it miraculously grow; shaping it to please the eye; taking delight in its warm aroma while it cooks; then revelling in the golden-crusted spectacle that emerges from the oven have all come to the fore again. The range-style cooker undoubtedly helps make this a pleasurable experience – no searching for a warm place for the bread to rise, no problems with warming tins and ingredients to just the right temperature and batch-baking is a doddle with roomy-sized ovens.

Place the flour and salt in a large bowl. Rub in the butter until the mixture resembles fine breadcrumbs. Make a well in the centre, crumble in the yeast then add the water. Mix with the hands to make a smooth dough. Turn out onto a lightly-floured surface and knead until smooth and elastic, about 5 minutes. Place in an oiled bowl and cover with cling film. Leave to rise in a warm place, ideally a surface near to the range, until doubled in size, about 1-1½ hours.

Turn the dough onto a lightly-floured surface, knock back to release all the air bubbles and knead again for about 4-5 minutes. Divide and then shape as required (see below). Place into warmed tins, cover with cling film and leave again near to the range until the dough has doubled in size and fills the tins, about 30 minutes.

Remove the cling film, glaze the loaves or rolls with beaten egg and sprinkle with seeds, if used.

2 **4** 2 OVEN RANGE AND 4 OVEN RANGE: Bake in the Roasting Oven with the grid shelf on the floor of the oven for about 25 minutes for the 450 g (1 lb) loaves, about 35-40 minutes for a 900 g (2 lb) loaf and 15-20 minutes for rolls, or until evenly browned.

 THERMODIAL-CONTROLLED RANGE: Bake in the oven set at 220°C/425°F for about 25 minutes for the 450 g (1 lb) loaves, about 35-40 minutes for a 900 g (2 lb) loaf and 15-20 minutes for rolls, or until evenly browned.

When they are cooked the loaves or rolls should sound hollow when rapped on the bottom with the knuckles. Allow to cool on a wire rack.

TO SHAPE LOAVES AND ROLLS

Tin Loaf: Flatten the whole dough, or half of the dough for two smaller loaves, to an oblong about 2.5 cm (1 inch) thick. Fold in three and tuck the ends over the seam. Place, seam-side down, in greased 450 g (1 lb) or 900 g (2 lb) tins. Cover and prove.

Split Tin: Shape the dough as for a tin loaf. Cover and leave to prove for 15 minutes. Make a deep slit lengthways down the centre of the loaf with a sharp knife. Cover and prove.

Cob: Knead the dough into a ball by drawing the dough upwards and into the centre. Place tucks side down on a greased baking tray. Cover and prove.

Latticed Cob: Shape the dough as for a cob loaf. Cover and leave to prove until almost doubled in size. With a sharp knife make a latticed effect over the top of the cob. Cover and leave to prove for a further 10 minutes.

Crown Loaf: Divide the dough into 12 equal pieces and knead each into a small ball. Place slightly apart in a greased 20 cm (8 inch) shallow round tin. Place about 9 around the edge of the tin and 3 in the centre. Cover and leave to prove.

Plait: Divide the dough into 3 equal pieces. Roll each into a long strand. Starting at the centre, plait the strands loosely together down to one end. Dampen the end of each strand and pinch together to seal. Plait the other end in the same way. Cover and prove.

Cottage Loaf: Cut off one third of the dough. Knead each piece of dough lightly into a ball. Place the larger round on a greased baking tray and slightly flatten the top. Place the smaller ball on top and prove until doubled in size. Push a floured wooden spoon handle through both the top and bottom balls of dough to make a hole in the centre of the loaf. Scissor snip around the top and bottom balls to give a notched cottage loaf if you prefer.

Round Rolls: Divide the dough into 12 equal pieces. Shape into rounds and place well apart on greased baking trays. Cover and prove.

Cloverleaf Rolls: Divide the dough into 12 equal pieces. Divide each piece into 3 again and shape into small balls. Place in groups of 3 in greased Yorkshire pudding tins or on greased trays. Cover and prove.

Finger or bridge rolls: Divide the dough into 12 equal pieces. Roll into sausage shapes. Place on greased baking trays. Cover and prove.

Coils: Divide the dough into 12 equal pieces. Roll each into a strand about 12-15 cm (4-5 inches) long. Curl up each like a spiral and place on greased baking trays. Cover and prove.

BUTTER BATCH ROLLS

MAKES 16

450 g (1 lb) plain flour

1 sachet 'easy-blend' or fast-action dried yeast

½ teaspoon salt

1 teaspoon caster sugar

175 ml (6 fl oz) milk

100 g (4 oz) butter, melted and cooled

1 egg, beaten

beaten egg to glaze

poppy or sesame seeds to sprinkle (optional)

 Slightly sweet, soft, spongy rolls that can be served for breakfast, lunch or tea. They freeze very well so can be made in batches when time is plentiful. To maximise both the flavour and texture, it is important that these rolls are served warm.

Mix the flour with the yeast, salt and sugar in a large bowl. Heat the milk until warm (about 43°C/110°F) then mix with butter and egg. Make a well in the centre of the flour mixture, add the butter mixture and mix to form a soft, but not sticky, dough. Knead on a lightly floured surface until smooth and elastic, about 5-10 minutes.

Divide the dough into 2 pieces. Working with one piece of dough, divide it evenly into 8 pieces. Form one into a round bun and place it in the centre of a greased 20 cm (8 inch) sandwich tin. Form 7 more buns from the remaining dough and place them around the central bun, leaving room to expand. Lightly cover with oiled polythene and leave on a surface near the range to prove until doubled in size. Repeat the whole procedure to make another tin of bread rolls.

Brush with beaten egg to glaze and sprinkle with seeds if using.

2 **4** 2 OVEN RANGE AND 4 OVEN RANGE: Bake in the Roasting Oven with the grid shelf on the floor of the oven for 15-20 minutes or until golden brown.

 THERMODIAL-CONTROLLED RANGE: Bake in the oven set at 220°C/ 425°F for about 15 minutes until golden brown.

Turn out and allow to cool on a wire rack.

SCOTTISH GIRDLE SPONGES

SERVES 4

25 g (1 oz) butter

1 tablespoon caster sugar

2 eggs, separated

100 g (4 oz) self-raising flour

pinch of salt

5 tablespoons milk

oil

 These are very light Scotch pancakes that can be cooked directly on the Simmering Plate. They are perfect for afternoon high tea or with fruit and cream as a dessert.

Cream the butter with the sugar until light and fluffy. Beat in the egg yolks. Sift the flour with the salt, add to the mixture with the milk and mix to make a thick creamy mixture. Whisk the egg whites until they stand in soft peaks and fold in gently with a metal spoon.

2 **4** **🌡** 2 OVEN RANGE, 4 OVEN RANGE, THERMODIAL-CONTROLLED RANGE: Grease the Simmering Plate lightly with oil removing any excess with absorbent kitchen paper and heat until just hazy. If the range is very hot then the Simmering Plate lid may need to be lifted first to allow the hotplate to cool a little before adding the oil and batter so that the sponges do not cook too fast and burn.

Drop tablespoons of the mixture onto the hot greased plate, spacing well apart and cook until the surfaces start to bubble. Turn over immediately with a palette knife and cook for a further 30 seconds. Transfer to a warmed plate and keep wrapped in a warm cloth while cooking the next batch. Serve warm.

MY ITALIAN FLOWERPOT LOAF

MAKES 1 LARGE LOAF

300 ml (½ pint) tepid water

1 tablespoon dried yeast

450 g (1 lb) strong plain unbleached bread flour

1 teaspoon salt

2 tablespoons finely chopped Pomodori Secchi (sun-dried tomatoes in sunflower oil)

1 tablespoon chopped green olives

1 clove garlic, finely chopped

2 tablespoons snipped chives

½ teaspoon chopped fresh thyme

25 g (1½ oz) toasted pine kernels

1 tablespoon olive oil

buckwheat to sprinkle (optional)

 I adore bread in all its guises and since it is something of a daily staple I constantly explore new ways of flavouring, shaping and serving it. This is the delicious result of a successful marriage between a basic yeast bread mixture and Italian sun-dried tomatoes, olives, garlic, herbs and pine nuts baked in a clay flowerpot. It is essential to use a well-scrubbed and oiled clay flowerpot with 1.35 litre (2¼ pint) capacity. You can line the pot with greased foil for easier release of the loaf.

Place half of the water in a bowl, sprinkle over the yeast and leave to stand in a warm place until frothy, about 10-15 minutes.

Mix the flour with the salt then stir in the yeast mixture, chopped tomatoes, olives, garlic, chives, thyme, pine kernels, oil and remaining warm water. Mix to a soft but manageable dough. Turn out onto a lightly floured surface and knead until elastic, about 5 minutes. Return to the bowl, cover with oiled polythene and leave on a surface near to the range to prove until doubled in size, about 1 hour.

Meanwhile, well oil a 1.35 litre (2¼ pint) clay flowerpot and leave to warm on the hob top.

Turn the dough onto a lightly floured surface and knead lightly for about 2 minutes then shape to fit the clay flowerpot. Cover with oiled polythene and leave on a surface near to the range until well-risen, about 40 minutes. Remove the oiled polythene and sprinkle with the buckwheat if using.

2 **4** 2 OVEN RANGE AND 4 OVEN RANGE: Bake in the Roasting Oven with the grid shelf on the floor of the oven for 35-40 minutes or until the loaf is well browned, has begun to shrink from the sides of the pot and makes a hollow sound when rapped on its base with your knuckles after removing from the pot.

THERMODIAL-CONTROLLED RANGE: Bake in the oven set at 200°C/ 400°F for 35-40 minutes or until the loaf is well browned, has begun to shrink from the sides of the pot and makes a hollow sound when rapped on its base with your knuckles after removing from the pot.

Allow to cool on a wire rack.

NOTE: Fast-action dried yeast may be used as an alternative. Simply mix 1 sachet with the flour then add the remaining ingredients and mix to a manageable dough. Knead for 5 minutes, then shape to fit the pot. Cover and leave to prove until well risen, about 40-60 minutes, then bake as above.

BASIC VICTORIA SANDWICH

MAKES 1 x 18 cm (7 inch) Sponge Cake

175 g (6 oz) margarine

175 g (6 oz) caster sugar

175 g (6 oz) self-raising flour

1½ teaspoons baking powder

3 large eggs (size 1 or 2)

4 tablespoons raspberry jam

150 ml (¼ pint) double cream, whipped (optional)

sifted icing sugar, to dust

 No home-baking chapter would be complete without a recipe for Victoria Sandwich. Whether you make the recipe by the all-in-one method or as I have done below the results will still be good. It is essential with 2 oven range models to place the cold plain shelf above the sponges during cooking in the Roasting Oven.

Cream the margarine with the sugar until light and fluffy. Sift the flour with the baking powder. Beat the eggs into the creamed mixture with a little of the flour. Carefully fold in the remaining flour. Line two 18 cm (7 inch) sandwich tins with greaseproof paper and divide the mixture equally between the tins, levelling the tops.

2 2 OVEN RANGE: Bake in the Roasting Oven with the grid shelf on the floor of the oven and the cold plain shelf on the second set of runners for about 20 minutes or until the tops spring back when lightly touched with the fingertips and the sponges are well-risen and golden brown.

4 4 OVEN RANGE: Bake in the Baking Oven with the grid shelf on the floor of the oven for about 20 minutes or until the tops spring back when lightly touched with the fingertips and the sponges are well-risen and golden brown.

THERMODIAL-CONTROLLED RANGE: Bake in the oven set at 180°C/350°F for about 20-25 minutes or until the tops spring back when lightly touched with the fingertips and the sponges are well-risen and golden brown.

Leave to cool in the tins for 2-3 minutes, then transfer to a wire rack to cool completely.

When cold remove the greaseproof paper and sandwich the cakes together with jam and cream and dust the top with icing sugar. Cut into wedges to serve.

VARIATIONS

LEMON OR ORANGE SANDWICH: Prepare as above but cream the margarine and sugar with the finely grated zest of 1 lemon or orange. Sandwich the cooled sponges with 4 tablespoons lemon or orange curd instead of the jam and cream.

COFFEE AND WALNUT SANDWICH: Prepare as above but cream the margarine and sugar with 4 teaspoons coffee and chicory essence or 2 heaped teaspoons instant coffee dissolved in a very small amount of hot water, and stir in 40 g (1½ oz) finely chopped walnuts with the flour. Sandwich the cooled sponges with cream whipped with 2-3 teaspoons coffee and chicory essence and omit the jam.

CHOCOLATE SANDWICH: Prepare as above but cream the margarine and sugar with 2 rounded tablespoons cocoa powder dissolved in 4 tablespoons hot water. Sandwich the cooled sponges with the cream and omit the jam.

SCONES FOR TEA

MAKES 12

225 g (8 oz) plain flour

1 tablespoon baking powder

½ teaspoon salt

50 g (2 oz) butter or margarine

25 g (1 oz) caster sugar

150 ml (¼ pint) milk

milk to glaze

 Nothing could be simpler or quicker to make and bake than a batch of scones for tea time. Whether you like them plain, studded with currants or sultanas or baked savoury fashion with cheese, ham or chives the recipe below will fit the bill.

Sift the flour, baking powder and salt into a bowl. Rub in the butter or margarine until the mixture resembles fine breadcrumbs. Stir in the sugar and milk and mix to a soft but manageable dough – take care not to overmix. Turn onto a lightly-floured surface and knead lightly until smooth.

Roll out the dough to about 2 cm (¾ inch) thick and stamp out 12 rounds with a 5-cm (2-inch) plain or fluted scone or biscuit cutter, re-rolling as necessary. Place on a greased baking sheet and glaze with milk.

 2 OVEN RANGE AND 4 OVEN RANGE: Cook in the Roasting Oven with the grid shelf on the third set of runners for about 10 minutes or until well-risen and golden.

THERMODIAL-CONTROLLED RANGE: Cook in the oven set at 220°C/425°F for about 10 minutes or until well-risen and golden.

Cool on a wire rack. Serve the scones with butter or whipped cream and jam or other sweet preserves. Store in an airtight tin until required.

VARIATIONS
FRUIT SCONES: Prepare as above, adding 40 g (1½ oz) currants or sultanas with the sugar.

CHEESE SCONES: Prepare as above, adding 1 teaspoon mustard powder and omitting the sugar. Mix in 50 g (2 oz) finely grated mature Cheddar cheese before adding the milk.

HAM AND CHIVE SCONES: Prepare as above, adding 1 teaspoon mustard powder and omitting the sugar. Mix in 25 g (1 oz) finely chopped cooked ham and 1 tablespoon snipped chives before adding the milk.

HONEY SCONES: Prepare as above, adding 1 tablespoon warmed clear honey and using only 7 tablespoons milk to bind the dough.

YOGURT OR SOURED CREAM SCONES: Prepare as above, substituting 4 tablespoons natural yogurt or soured cream for 4 tablespoons of the milk. Omit the sugar if a savoury scone is required.

BUTTERMILK SCONES: Prepare as above, using 150 ml (¼ pint) buttermilk instead of the milk.

HONEYED CARROT, PINEAPPLE AND WALNUT CAKE

MAKES: 1 x 18 cm (7 inch) round cake

Cake

1 x 220 g (7½ oz) can pineapple slices
225 g (8 oz) plain flour
½ teaspoon salt
¾ teaspoon bicarbonate of soda
1 teaspoon baking powder
½ teaspoon ground cinnamon
100 g (4 oz) granulated sugar
2½ tablespoons set honey
2 eggs, beaten
5 tablespoons oil
4 large carrots, finely grated
25 g (1 oz) walnuts, chopped

Frosting

225 g (8 oz) icing sugar
40 g (1½ oz) butter
40 g (1½ oz) cream cheese or quark
½ teaspoon vanilla essence
walnut halves, to decorate

This is a super carrot cake made doubly delicious with the addition of chopped pineapple and walnuts. I like to use walnut oil in the mixture but sunflower or vegetable oil is also suitable.

Drain the juice from the pineapple and reserve to use in the frosting. Place the pineapple slices in a food processor or blender and process until finely chopped or finely chop by hand. Sift the flour with the salt, bicarbonate of soda, baking powder and cinnamon. Add the sugar, honey, eggs, oil, carrots, walnuts and pineapple. Mix well until thoroughly blended. Spoon into a greased and lined 18-cm (7-inch) deep round cake tin.

2 2 OVEN RANGE: Place the tin on the grid shelf on the floor of the Roasting Oven with the cold plain shelf on the second set of runners above the cake. Bake until the top of the cake is set and an even golden-brown colour, about 20 minutes. Transfer the hot plain shelf to the centre of the Simmering Oven, place the half-cooked cake on top of it and continue to bake until cooked, about 1 hour.

4 4 OVEN RANGE: Place the tin on the grid shelf on the floor of the Baking Oven and cook for about 1 hour 20 minutes.

 THERMODIAL-CONTROLLED RANGE: Place the tin in the centre of the oven set at 180°C/350°F and cook for 1 hour 20 minutes.

The cake is cooked when a skewer inserted into the centre of the cake comes out clean of mixture. Cool on a wire rack.

To make the frosting, place the ingredients in a bowl with 1-2 teaspoons of the reserved pineapple juice and beat until smooth. Spread and swirl over the top and sides of the cake. Decorate with walnut halves to serve.

SPECIAL RICH CELEBRATION FRUIT CAKE

I have made this recipe countless times as the base for a Christmas cake or for a special celebration cake. Just recently I made it for my grandmother's 80th birthday party and it was just as good as ever – rich, fruity and moist. Since the Simmering Oven temperature can vary slightly over a long period of time check the condition of the cake after three-quarters of the recommended cooking time and regularly after that for success.

Cream the butter with the sugar until light and fluffy. Beat in the lemon rind and eggs, a little at a time, adding a little flour if the mixture starts to curdle. Sift the flour with the spice and cinnamon and fold into the creamed mixture. Fold in the fruit, nuts and brandy, mixing well. Spoon into the greased and greaseproof paper-lined tin and level the surface.

2 **4** 🌡 2 OVEN RANGE, 4 OVEN RANGE, THERMODIAL-CONTROLLED RANGE: Cook in the Simmering Oven with the grid shelf on the floor of the oven for the following recommended time:

Cake Size	Butter	Brown Sugar	Lemon Rind	Eggs (Size 1, 2)	Plain Flour	Mixed Spice	Cinnamon	Dried Fruit	Glacé Cherries	Mixed Peel	Almonds	Brandy	Cooking Time
15-cm (6-inch) square or 8-cm (7-inch) round	175g (6oz)	175g (6oz)	¼ lemon	3	210g (7½oz)	½ tsp	½ tsp	600g (1lb 5oz)	75g (3oz)	50g (2oz)	50g (2oz)	1 tbsp	8 hours
18-cm (7-inch) square or 20-cm (8-inch) round	250g (9oz)	250g (9oz)	¼ lemon	5	300g (11oz)	¾ tsp	¾ tsp	925g (2lb 10oz)	150g (5oz)	75g (3oz)	75g (3oz)	1½ tbsp	10 hours
20-cm (8-inch) square or 23-cm (9-inch) round	350g (12oz)	350g (14oz)	½ lemon	6	400g (14oz)	1 tsp	1 tsp	1.075 kg (2lb 6oz)	175g (6oz)	100g (4oz)	100g (4oz)	2 tbsp	11 hours
23-cm (9-inch) square or 25-cm (10-inch) round	500g (1lb 2oz)	500g (1lb 2oz)	½ lemon	9	600g (1lb 5oz)	1 tsp	1 tsp	1.525kg (3lb 6oz)	250g (9oz)	150g (5oz)	150g (5oz)	2-3 tbsp	12 hours
25-cm (10-inch) square or 28-cm (11-inch) round	600g (1lb 5oz)	600g (1lb 5oz)	½ lemon	11	675g (1lb 8oz)	2 tsp	2 tsp	1.9kg (4lb 4oz)	275g (10oz)	200g (7oz)	200g (7oz)	3 tbsp	13 hours
28-cm (11-inch) square or 30-cm (12-inch) round	800g (1lb 12oz)	800g (1lb 12oz)	½ lemon	14	825g (1lb 13oz)	2½ tsp	2½ tsp	2.475kg (5lb 8oz)	350g (12oz)	250g (9oz)	250g (9oz)	4 tbsp	14 hours
30-cm (12-inch) square or 33-cm (13-inch) round	950g (2lb 2oz)	950g (2lb 2oz)	1 lemon	17	1.075kg (2lb 6oz)	2½ tsp	2½ tsp	2.925kg (6lb 8oz)	425g (15oz)	275g (10oz)	275g (10oz)	6 tbsp	15 hours

To test if the cake is cooked insert a warm skewer into the centre of the cake. If it comes out clean of mixture then the cake is cooked. If the skewer comes out with a tackiness of mixture clinging to it then cook for a further 30 minutes before testing again. Allow to cool in the tin. When cold wrap in foil and store in an airtight tin until required.

CINNAMON AND HONEY GLAZED CHOUX BUNS

MAKES 12-14

Choux Pastry

50 g (2 oz) butter or margarine

150 ml (¼ pint) water

65 g (2½ oz) plain flour

pinch of salt

2 eggs, beaten

Filling

200 g (7 oz) fromage frais with strawberries

about 6 strawberries, sliced

Glaze

2 tablespoons clear honey

large pinch of ground cinnamon

 Deliciously crisp, yet creamy and shiny glazed choux buns are filled in this recipe with strawberries and fromage frais. Wonderful as a teatime treat!

Melt the butter or margarine in a pan with the water then slowly bring to the boil. Remove from the heat and quickly add all of the flour and salt and beat with a wooden spoon until the mixture forms a ball and leaves the sides of the pan clean. Allow to cool slightly then gradually beat in the eggs to make a smooth and glossy paste. Spoon into a piping bag fitted with a large plain nozzle. Pipe about 12-14 balls onto a greased baking sheet leaving room between each for the mixture to rise.

2 **4** 2 OVEN RANGE AND 4 OVEN RANGE: Place the sheet on the grid shelf set on the lowest set of runners in the Roasting Oven for about 20 minutes until light golden brown. Make a small slit in the side of each bun to allow the steam to escape. Transfer to the Simmering Oven and cook for about 20 minutes until crisp, golden and dry on the inside.

 THERMODIAL-CONTROLLED RANGE: Place the sheet in the centre of the oven set at 200°C/400°F and cook for 15 minutes. Reduce the oven temperature to 180°C/350°F. Make a small slit in the side of each bun to allow the steam to escape. Return to the oven and cook for a further 15-20 minutes until crisp, golden and dry on the inside.

Allow to cool completely then split and fill with the fromage frais and slices of strawberry.

Heat the honey with the cinnamon until hot and bubbly then brush over the tops of the buns. Cool slightly, then brush again with the glaze to coat. Allow to cool completely before serving.

CRANBERRY, APPLE AND PEAR FILO STRUDELS

SERVES 4

1 eating apple, peeled, cored and thinly sliced

 Wonderful pastries to make when the days grow autumnal, then wintery and there is still a good crop of tree fruits, like apples and pears to use alongside the new import of bright red cranberries.

50 g (2 oz) fresh cranberries

50-75 g (2-3 oz) caster sugar

50 g (2 oz) fresh white breadcrumbs

50 g (2 oz) raisins

1 teaspoon ground cinnamon

4 large leaves filo pastry

melted butter and oil to brush

1 large pear, peeled, cored and cut into quarters

icing sugar, to dust

Place the apple, cranberries, sugar and a little water in a pan and cook gently until the cranberries 'pop'. Add the breadcrumbs, raisins and cinnamon and mix well. Take one leaf of filo pastry, brush liberally with melted butter and oil, fold in half and brush again. Place one quarter of the cranberry mixture in the middle of the pastry square and place a piece of pear on top. Fold the sides of the pastry over the filling and form a small parcel or gather up the sides and twist in the centre to make a money bag shape. Transfer to a lightly greased baking sheet and repeat, using the remaining cranberry mixture, pastry and pears. Brush each parcel or money bag with the melted butter and oil to coat.

2 **4** 2 OVEN RANGE AND 4 OVEN RANGE: With the grid shelf on the floor of the oven, cook for about 20-25 minutes until lightly golden and crisp, turning the sheet around once for even browning.

THERMODIAL-CONTROLLED RANGE: Place in the oven set at 180°C/350°F and bake for 20-30 minutes until lightly golden and crisp.

Serve hot or cold, dusted with icing sugar.

CINNAMON MACAROONS

MAKES ABOUT 12

1 egg white

50 g (2 oz) ground almonds

50 g (2 oz) caster sugar

½ teaspoon ground cinnamon

a few flaked or split almonds, for decoration

 I like to serve small macaroons with strong black coffee after a meal and to bury them with fruit and sabayon in sophisticated trifles so there always seems to be a batch just cooked. The ones here have a hint of cinnamon so they also go especially well with apple-based desserts.

Whisk the egg white until stiff then fold in the ground almonds, sugar and cinnamon with a metal spoon. Place teaspoonfuls of the mixture onto a large baking sheet lined with rice paper. Decorate with a few flaked or split almonds.

2 2 OVEN RANGE: Cook in the Roasting Oven with the grid shelf on the lowest set of runners and with the cold plain shelf above for about 15 minutes or until firm to the touch and crisp.

4 4 OVEN RANGE: Cook in the Baking Oven with the grid shelf on the third set of runners for about 15-20 minutes or until firm to the touch and crisp.

 THERMODIAL-CONTROLLED RANGE: Cook in the oven set at 180°C/350°F for about 15-20 minutes or until firm to the touch and crisp.

Remove from the sheet when cold and trim away the rice paper from the macaroon edges before serving.

NUTTY OAT AND FRUIT COOKIES

MAKES 40

275 g (10 oz) raisins

100 ml (4 fl oz) boiling water

75 g (3 oz) unsalted butter

175 g (6 oz) light brown sugar

½ teaspoon vanilla essence

1 large egg (size 1 or 2), lightly beaten

275 g (10 oz) plain flour

¼ teaspoon baking powder

¾ teaspoon bicarbonate of soda

½ teaspoon salt

1 teaspoon ground cinnamon

½ teaspoon ground cloves

100 g (3½ oz) rolled oats

100 g (4 oz) chopped walnuts

175 g (6 oz) chopped stoned prunes

My children really like these cookies that are bursting with fruit, nuts and spice. They make a good lunch box or picnic extra to cope with fresh-air sharpened appetites.

Place the raisins in a small bowl and pour over the boiling water. Cover and leave to stand for 30 minutes. Drain, reserving 2 tablespoons of the liquid.

Cream the butter with the sugar and vanilla essence until light and fluffy then beat in the egg.

Sift the flour with the baking powder, bicarbonate of soda, salt, cinnamon and cloves. Gradually add to the creamed mixture with the reserved soaking liquid. Stir in the raisins, oats, walnuts and prunes.

Drop spoonfuls of the prepared cookie mixture onto greased baking sheets, flattening the mounds lightly with the back of the spoon.

2 4 2 OVEN RANGE AND 4 OVEN RANGE: Cook, in batches, in the Roasting Oven with the grid shelf on the second set of runners for about 7-8 minutes, or until golden.

 THERMODIAL-CONTROLLED RANGE: Cook, in batches, in the oven set at 200°C/400°F for about 7-8 minutes, or until golden.

Transfer to a rack to cool. Store in an airtight tin until required.

CHOC-ORANGE FINGERS

MAKES ABOUT 36

75 g (3 oz) plain flour

2 tablespoons cornflour

⅛ teaspoon baking powder

pinch of salt

100 g (4 oz) unsalted butter

40 g (1½ oz) icing sugar, sifted

1 large egg (size 1 or 2), separated

2 tablespoons grated orange zest

¼ teaspoon vanilla essence

1 tablespoon fresh orange juice

granulated sugar, to sprinkle

50 g (2 oz) plain dessert chocolate, melted

These are melt-in-the-mouth biscuit fingers flavoured with orange and dipped in melted chocolate. They are ideal for serving with tea or coffee but are also lovely to serve with special desserts.

Sift the flour with the cornflour, baking powder and salt. Cream the butter with the icing sugar until light and fluffy. Beat in the egg yolk, orange zest, vanilla essence and orange juice. Stir in the flour mixture and mix well.

Whisk the egg white until it forms soft peaks then fold into the mixture to make a soft dough. Spoon into a piping bag fitted with nozzle with a decorative ribbon tip. Pipe 4 cm (1½ inch) lengths onto greased baking sheets about 2.5 cm (1 inch) apart to allow for spreading. Sprinkle with a little granulated sugar.

2 2 OVEN RANGE: Bake in the Roasting Oven, in batches, with the grid shelf on the lowest set of runners and the cold plain shelf above for about 10-12 minutes, or until the edges are golden.

4 4 OVEN RANGE: Bake in the Baking Oven, in batches, with the grid shelf on the third set of runners for about 10-12 minutes, or until the edges are golden.

THERMODIAL-CONTROLLED RANGE: Cook in batches in the oven set at 180°C/350°F for about 10-12 minutes, or until the edges are golden.

Transfer to a wire rack to cool. When completely cold, dip one end of each biscuit in the melted chocolate to coat. Return to the rack to allow the chocolate to cool and harden.

DRINKS, PRESERVES AND SPECIAL GIFTS

CRANBERRY HOT TODDY

SERVES 8-10

2 x 680 ml (23 fl oz) bottles
Cranberry and Raspberry Juice
Drink

---

1 large bottle ginger ale

---

1 cinnamon stick

---

1 teaspoon ground ginger

---

1 teaspoon Angostura Bitters

---

a selection of sliced fruit

Here's a simple recipe for a non-alcoholic hot toddy that even the children can enjoy at Hallow'een or on Bonfire night.

2 **4** 🌡 2 OVEN RANGE, 4 OVEN RANGE, THERMODIAL-CONTROLLED RANGE: Place all the ingredients in a large heavy-based pan and heat through slowly on the Simmering Plate but do not allow to boil. Leave to cool slightly before pouring into a punch bowl. Float a selection of sliced fruit on top. Ladle into heatproof glasses to serve.

POSITIVELY POTENT PUNCH

MAKES about 1.35 litres (2¼ pints)

1 standard bottle red wine

---

600 ml (1 pint) medium cider

---

3 tablespoons honey

---

3 teaspoons whole allspice

---

2 cinnamon sticks

---

2 tablespoons brown rum

---

apple and orange slices

Certainly not a drink for the children, this party punch can deliver quite a kick especially since it tastes so innocent!

2 **4** 🌡 2 OVEN RANGE, 4 OVEN RANGE, THERMODIAL-CONTROLLED RANGE: Place the wine, cider, honey, allspice and cinnamon sticks in a large heavy-based pan. Heat on the Simmering Plate to just below boiling point for about 10 minutes.

Add the rum then remove the spices with a slotted spoon. Add the slices of fruit to garnish and serve warm in heatproof glasses.

ICED MINT SODA

**MAKES 600 ml (1 pint)
mint syrup**

about 25 mint leaves

225 g (8 oz) granulated sugar

250 ml (8 fl oz) boiling water

 This is a recipe for a super cool mint syrup that is then topped up with sparkling mineral water, soda or lemonade for a refreshing summer drink. If you haven't got a pestle and mortar, bruise the mint leaves and sugar in a bowl with the end of a rolling pin.

 2 OVEN RANGE, 4 OVEN RANGE, THERMODIAL-CONTROLLED RANGE: Place the mint leaves and sugar in a large pestle and mortar and bruise the leaves so that they flavour the sugar.

Place in a large pan with the water and cook on the Simmering Plate until the sugar dissolves. Bring to the boil and simmer for 3-5 minutes to make a rich minty syrup.

Strain, cool and pour into a sterilised bottle and cork.

To serve, fill a tall glass with crushed ice, add the mint syrup to taste and top up with mineral water, soda water or lemonade.

RASPBERRY VINEGAR

**MAKES about 600 ml
(1 pint)**

450 g (1 lb) raspberries, hulled

600 ml (1 pint) wine or
distilled vinegar

450 g (1 lb) white or brown
sugar

 A wonderful fruity vinegar that is so good in salad dressings but also when diluted makes a refreshing summer drink. I often add a bottle to a gourmet food basket for giving at Christmas.

Wash the fruit and place in a large bowl. Crush with the back of a wooden spoon and add the vinegar, mixing well. Cover and leave to stand for 4-5 days, stirring occasionally.

2 OVEN RANGE, 4 OVEN RANGE, THERMODIAL-CONTROLLED RANGE: Strain through muslin into a saucepan and add the sugar, mixing well. Heat gently to dissolve, then bring to the boil and boil gently for 10 minutes.

Allow to cool, strain again and pour into clean warm bottles, leaving a 2.5 cm (1 inch) headspace. You can add a few whole washed raspberries to the bottle. Seal securely with vinegar-proof tops, label and store in a cool, dark place for up to 2 weeks before using.

VARIATIONS
REDCURRANT VINEGAR: Prepare and cook as above, but use 450 g (1 lb) topped and tailed redcurrants instead of the raspberries.

BLACKBERRY VINEGAR: Prepare and cook as above, but use 450 g (1 lb) hulled blackberries instead of the raspberries.

BLACKCURRANT VINEGAR: Prepare and cook as above, but use 450 g (1 lb) topped and tailed blackcurrants instead of the raspberries.

GINGER AND MINT STIR FRY OIL

MAKES 1.2 litres (2 pints)

2.5 cm (1 inch) piece root ginger, peeled and thinly sliced

1.2 litres (2 pints) sunflower oil

small handful (about 8 sprigs) fresh mint

2 dried red chillis, broken into small pieces

I buy all sorts of flavoured oils for cooking – chilli, sesame, lemon, herb and truffle but this is one I make myself especially for stir frying or for adding to a salad dressing.

 2 OVEN RANGE, 4 OVEN RANGE, THERMODIAL-CONTROLLED RANGE: Place the ginger and oil in a pan and heat gently on the Simmering Plate until very hot but not boiling. Allow to cool then strain to remove the ginger.

Divide the mint sprigs and red chillis between two 600 ml (1 pint) clean, dry bottles and fill with the ginger-flavoured oil. Screw on the caps and leave to stand in a sunny place (a window sill is ideal) for 2 weeks. Use immediately.

For longer term storage, strain the oil and discard the mint leaves and chillis. Re-bottle, seal and store in a cool place.

SPICED FRUIT FUDGE

MAKES ABOUT 60

100 g (4 oz) butter

300 ml (½ pint) milk

900 g (2 lb) granulated sugar

1 x 198 g (7 oz) can sweetened condensed milk

1 teaspoon ground mixed spice

175 g (6 oz) raisins

Whether you need a tray of fudge for a charity bazaar, school fête or just for eating at home then this recipe is a delicious and reliable one. Do use a very large pan, about 4 litre (7 pint) capacity when making since the mixture bubbles high and can splash.

2 4 2 OVEN RANGE, 4 OVEN RANGE, THERMODIAL-CONTROLLED RANGE: Place the butter and milk in a large heavy-based pan. Heat gently on the Simmering Plate until the butter has melted. Add the sugar and stir over a low heat until dissolved.

Stir in the condensed milk and slowly bring the mixture to the boil. Continue to boil on the Simmering Plate, stirring frequently, for about 20 minutes or until the mixture begins to thicken and turn a caramel colour. Remove from the heat and allow to cool until the mixture starts to thicken and crystallise.

Add the mixed spice and raisins and beat the mixture vigorously for about 5 minutes or until it becomes very thick.

Pour into a greased shallow baking tin about 18 x 28 cm (7 x 11 inches) and leave to set. When firm mark into small squares. Cut when completely cold. Store in an airtight tin until required.

LEMON AND PISTACHIO TURKISH DELIGHT

MAKES 64

450 ml (¾ pint) water

3 x 11 g (0.4 oz) sachets of powdered gelatine

675 g (1½ lb) granulated sugar

grated rind and juice of 1 lemon

50 g (2 oz) shelled pistachios, coarsely chopped

25 g (1 oz) icing sugar, sifted

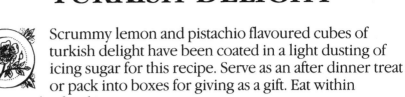

Scrummy lemon and pistachio flavoured cubes of turkish delight have been coated in a light dusting of icing sugar for this recipe. Serve as an after dinner treat or pack into boxes for giving as a gift. Eat within one month of making.

2 **4** 🌡 2 OVEN RANGE, 4 OVEN RANGE, THERMODIAL-CONTROLLED RANGE: Place the water in a large heavy-based pan and heat until warm. Remove from the heat and sprinkle over the gelatine, stirring until dissolved. Stir in the sugar, return to the Simmering Plate and heat gently until the sugar has dissolved, stirring frequently. Bring to the boil and boil for 20 minutes or until the mixture is thick and syrupy. *DO NOT STIR.*

Remove from the heat and leave to stand for 10 minutes. Carefully remove any scum from the surface of the mixture with a spoon then leave to cool until beginning to set, about 5-10 minutes.

Stir in the lemon rind, lemon juice and pistachios, mixing well. Pour into a 20-cm (8-inch) loose-bottomed square tin lined with non-stick baking parchment and chill until cold and set, at least 6 hours.

To serve, invert the turkish delight onto a surface dusted with half of the icing sugar, peel off the baking parchment and cut into 2.5-cm (1-inch) squares. Sprinkle over the remaining sugar and roll the squares in the sugar so that they are coated on all sides. Transfer to a plate to serve or put in a decorative box with extravagant bow to give as a gift.

SPICY NUT AND SEED NIBBLES

2 tablespoons oil

15 g (½ oz) butter

450 g (1 lb) mixed shelled nuts (peanuts, cashews, almonds, hazelnuts, pistachios and brazils for example)

4 tablespoons mixed seeds (sunflower and sesame seeds for example)

2 teaspoons mild curry powder

These are lovely to serve with drinks but make a splendid gift for an uncle, grandfather or hard-to-suit male member of the family when Christmas comes around. Ideally pack in an airtight container to keep fresh and crisp.

2 **4** 🌡 2 OVEN RANGE, 4 OVEN RANGE, THERMODIAL-CONTROLLED RANGE: Heat the oil and butter in a large frying pan, add the nuts and seeds and cook, over a moderate heat, until lightly browned on all sides, stirring frequently. Add the curry powder, mixing well and cook for a further 2 minutes. Remove from the pan and spread out onto a tray to cool completely. Store in an airtight tin until required.

GINGER AND COCONUT TRUFFLES

MAKES ABOUT 25

175 g (6 oz) good-quality plain dessert chocolate

50 g (2 oz) unsalted butter

175 g (6 oz) ginger snaps or thins, crushed

25 g (1 oz) desiccated coconut

50 g (2 oz) stem ginger, finely chopped

1 tablespoon ginger wine

powdered chocolate or cocoa to coat

Delicious little truffles that are child's play to make but more importantly keep well since they do not contain lashings of cream like so many other rich truffle mixtures. They are perfect to give as a gift if placed in small cases and boxed or placed in cellophane and tied with a decorative ribbon.

2 **4** 🌡 2 OVEN RANGE, 4 OVEN RANGE, THERMODIAL-CONTROLLED RANGE: Break the chocolate into a bowl, add the butter and place over a pan of just simmering water and stir until smooth and melted.

Remove from the heat add the biscuit crumbs, coconut, ginger and ginger wine and mix well. Allow to cool slightly then chill until the mixture thickens and becomes firm.

Divide and shape the mixture into about 25 small balls. Roll in powdered chocolate or cocoa powder to coat and place in small sweet cases. Store in a cool place until required.

GARLIC, THYME AND OLIVES PRESERVED IN OIL

MAKES 1 JAR

4-6 heads garlic, depending upon size of garlic and jar used for preserving

good quality olive oil, to cover

4-6 sprigs fresh thyme

about 10-12 black olives

1 bay leaf

Whole heads of new-season garlic and sprigs of fresh thyme are highly prized by cooks when preserved in oil for autumn and winter use. The garlic and olives are excellent when added to soups, casseroles and hot pots or to gratin-style dishes. The herb and garlic flavoured oil is splendid for drizzling over roasts and grills or for use in salad dressings.

Carefully peel away the papery outer layers of the garlic cloves but keeping the whole head intact. Place on a large sheet of greaseproof paper lightly brushed with oil. Fold up the edges of the paper to completely enclose the garlic and place in a roasting tin.

2 **4** 2 OVEN RANGE AND 4 OVEN RANGE: Bake in the Roasting Oven with the grid shelf on the lowest set of runners for about 15-20 minutes or until the cloves are tender.

THERMODIAL-CONTROLLED RANGE: Bake in the oven set at 190°C/ 375°F for about 15-20 minutes or until the cloves are tender.

Unwrap the garlic from the paper parcel and place in a wide-necked preserving jar. Tuck the sprigs of thyme between each with the black olives. Pour in enough olive oil to cover and top with the bay leaf. Securely cover the top of the jar with the lid and store in a cold place for 2 months before using.

THE ONLY MINT SAUCE

MAKES ABOUT
600 ml (1 pint)

275 g (10 oz) fresh mint, washed, dried and finely chopped

450 g (1 lb) granulated sugar

600 ml (1 pint) vinegar

So many commercial preserves these days taste bland, artificial or simply lack real intense flavour. Mint sauce is often one of the worst offenders so I insist that we make our own during the early summer months to last the year round. Needless to say it has become the 'only' mint sauce we have. It is essential to use only young, tender fresh mint leaves. Wash them, discarding the stalks and dry on absorbent kitchen paper, then chop finely on a board or, for speed, in a food processor.

2 OVEN RANGE, 4 OVEN RANGE, THERMODIAL-CONTROLLED RANGE: Pack the mint into dry, wide-necked small preserving jars. Place the sugar and vinegar in a pan and heat slowly to dissolve the sugar, then bring to the boil.

Pour over the mint and seal with airtight covers. Store in a cool, dry place for 1 month before using and up to 1 year.

To use, remove from the jar about 1 tablespoon of the concentrated mint sauce per person, and place in a bowl. Add a little extra vinegar and salt and pepper to taste, blending well. Serve in a sauceboat – a favourite with lamb but a good addition to a salad dressing.

A TRIO OF CURDS

**MAKES ABOUT 675 g
(1½ lb) or 3 small pots**

100 g (4 oz) butter

225 g (8 oz) caster sugar

finely grated rind and juice of 3
lemons or limes OR finely
grated rind and juice of 2 small
oranges and 1 lemon

3 eggs

1 egg yolk

 Lemon, lime and orange curd are some of the most delicious preserves I know for serving with sweet breads, to fill a sponge sandwich or to flavour or top ice cream. I often make a batch to use up leftover egg yolks after making meringues and give a few pots away as gifts since their fresh flavours are always appreciated.

2 **4** 🌡 2 OVEN RANGE, 4 OVEN RANGE, THERMODIAL-CONTROLLED RANGE: Place the butter and sugar in a heatproof bowl and place over a pan of simmering water. Heat, stirring frequently, until the butter melts.

Add the fruit rind and juice and mix well. Beat the eggs with the egg yolk and add to the mixture, blending well. Continue to cook, stirring frequently, until the curd thickens and will coat the back of a wooden spoon, about 25-30 minutes. Do not overcook or allow the mixture to boil or the mixture will separate.

Remove from the heat and pour or ladle into warm, clean jars. Cover, seal and label. Store in a cool place for up to 2 weeks or in the refrigerator for up to 2 months.

LEMON AND CORIANDER PICKLE

**MAKES ABOUT
4 x 450 g (1 lb) jars**

900 g (2 lb) lemons

75 g (3 oz) root ginger

15 g (½ oz) green chillies

2 tablespoons coriander
berries

675 g (1½ lb) granulated sugar

150 ml (¼ pint) white wine
vinegar

1½ tablespoons sea salt

This is an excellent pickle to serve with rich cold meats such as pork or duck but equally good with cheese and bread. If you don't care for the flavour of coriander then use 2 teaspoons mustard seed instead of the coriander berries. Choose thin-skinned lemons that feel heavy to the hand since they will be more juicy than thick-skinned ones. Cooking time will depend upon the thickness of the lemon skins – from 40 minutes to 1¼ hours.

Wash and dry the lemons. Cut into eighths and remove the pips. Peel and finely chop the root ginger. If you don't want the pickle to be too hot then split and remove the seeds from the chillies, otherwise leave whole.

Place the lemons, ginger, chillies, coriander berries, sugar, wine vinegar and salt in a large bowl and mix well. Cover and keep refrigerated for 4 days, turning the mixture occasionally.

2 **4** 🌡 2 OVEN RANGE, 4 OVEN RANGE, THERMODIAL-CONTROLLED RANGE: Transfer to a large heavy-based pan, bring to the boil, transfer to the Simmering Plate and simmer gently until thick and syrupy, about 40 minutes or longer if the lemon skins are thick.

Pour into warm, clean, dry jars and seal. Label and store until required for up to a year.

TUDOR DAMSON JAM

**MAKES ABOUT 4.5 kg
(10 lb)**

2.1 kg (4¾ lb) damsons

900 ml (1½ pints) water

2.7 kg (6 lb) preserving sugar

knob of butter

No, this isn't a very old jam recipe but my name for the damson jam made from the fruit of a tree that stands in the courtyard of our house, Tudor Court. Year after year it never fails to give us a huge basketful of damsons, which we nearly always make into jam. As I sit here writing out this recipe I can see its boughs heavily-laden with creamy white blossom so it looks like we might get a bumper harvest again. Predictably Tudor Damson Jam has something of a reputation amongst friends and family! Try the recipe yourself – you won't be disappointed.

2 **4** 🌡 2 OVEN RANGE, 4 OVEN RANGE, THERMODIAL-CONTROLLED RANGE: Wash the damsons and place in a large preserving or heavy-based pan with the water. Bring to the boil, reduce the heat and simmer until tender, about 20-30 minutes.

Add the sugar, mixing well. Heat gently to dissolve the sugar, stirring occasionally. Add the butter to reduce foaming. Bring to the boil and boil rapidly until setting point is reached, about 10-20 minutes. Remove the damson stones with a slotted spoon and discard. Remove from the heat and skim if necessary.

Spoon into clean, hot jars, cover with waxed discs, waxed-sides down, and dampened cellophane rounds. Label and store in a cool, dry, dark place for up to a year.

APPLE AND ROSEMARY JELLY

**MAKES ABOUT
3.25 kg (7 lb)**

2.25 kg (5 lb) cooking apples

600 ml (1 pint) water

4 tablespoons fresh rosemary leaves, washed and dried

250 ml (8 fl oz) distilled vinegar

preserving sugar (see method)

The best savoury jelly I know to serve with roast lamb, grilled fish and game birds. Make lots so that you can give pots away at Harvest Festival celebrations or Christmas.

2 **4** 🌡 2 OVEN RANGE, 4 OVEN RANGE, THERMODIAL-CONTROLLED RANGE: Coarsely chop or slice the apples (without coring) into a preserving pan or large heavy-based pan. Add the water and half of the rosemary, mixing well. Bring to the boil, reduce the heat and simmer gently until very soft, about 40-50 minutes. Add the vinegar, mixing well, and boil for a further 5 minutes.

Spoon into a jelly bag and leave to strain into a bowl for at least 12 hours.

Measure the juice and return to the pan. Add 450 g (1 lb) warmed sugar for each 600 ml (1 pint) measured juice. Heat gently to dissolve the sugar, bring to the boil and boil rapidly until setting point is reached, about 10 minutes.

Skim if necessary, stir in the remaining rosemary, finely chopped and mix well. Allow to cool slightly, stir well and spoon into clean, hot jars. Cover with waxed discs, waxed-sides down, and dampened cellophane rounds. Label and store in a cool, dry, dark place for up to a year.

BOTTLING IN THE RANGE

Making your own bottled preserves, either from home-grown, farm-picked or shop-bought fruits is great fun, and a few shelves of really individual preserves and bottled fruits are an infinite source of satisfaction, variety and inspiration the whole year round. I use Kilner preserving jars for bottling fruits in my Aga. There are two types; glass-lidded jars secured by a metal clip or glass-lidded jars with colourful polypropylene screwbands, which also have the bonus of making preserved fruits ideal to give as thoughtful culinary gifts.

A FEW GOLDEN RULES BEFORE YOU BEGIN

- Before use, check that all jars and fittings are in good condition.

- Check that jars are absolutely clean, wash them well and rinse in clean hot water.

- Soak the rubber rings in hot water for a few minutes then bring them to the boil before use.

- Don't use a rubber ring more than once – spares can be easily and cheaply bought from a local stockist.

- Never attempt to preserve vegetables by bottling – the temperatures reached are not high enough for safe preservation.

- Choose fruit that is sound, fresh, clean and properly ripe – neither too soft nor too hard.

- Choose fruits of a similar shape, size and ripeness for any one jar.

The method recommended for bottling fruits using a range-style cooker is the oven method where fruit is preserved in a sugar syrup. The sugar syrup is made from 225 g (8 oz) sugar to 600 ml (1 pint) water. Generally, fruit is packed, layer by layer, in clean jars then filled up with syrup before processing.

Warm the jars and fill with the fruit. Fill the jars to within 2.5 cm (1 inch) of the tops with boiling syrup. Fit the rubber rings around the inside of the glass lids and place on the jars ensuring that the rubber rings lie evenly all round. Do not fix screwbands or metal clips.

2 **4** 2 OVEN RANGE AND 4 OVEN RANGE: Place the jars in the Simmering Oven on a roasting tin or baking tray lined with a few sheets of newspaper and cook for the time recommended in the chart.

Cooking times vary according to the fruit being bottled, its ripeness and size, the number of bottles being preserved and the size of the jars. The chart below is given as a guide. For best results do not preserve more than 6-8 bottles at any one time or the fruit may bottle too slowly and discolour. Remember too that those bottles at the back of the oven will cook faster than those at the front so may need removing first or re-arranging for even cooking.

1-2 jars	1 hour
3-6 jars	2-3 hours
7-8 jars	2½-3½ hours

THERMODIAL-CONTROLLED RANGE: Cook in the oven set at 150°C/ 300°F on a roasting tin or baking tray lined with a few sheets of newspaper and cook for the time recommended in the chart.

FRUIT	TIME IN MINUTES
Apples, sliced	30-40 minutes
Apricots, halved	50-60 minutes
Apricots, whole	40-50 minutes
Blackberries	30-40 minutes
Cherries, whole	40-50 minutes
Currants	30-40 minutes
Damsons, whole	40-50 minutes
Figs	60-70 minutes
Gages, whole	55-70 minutes
Gooseberries	45-60 minutes
Loganberries	45-60 minutes
Mulberries	45-60 minutes
Nectarines, halved	65-80 minutes
Peaches, halved	65-80 minutes
Pears	60-70 minutes
Plums, halved	65-80 minutes
Plums, whole	55-70 minutes
Raspberries	45-60 minutes
Rhubarb	40-50 minutes
Strawberries	50-60 minutes
Tomatoes, whole	60-70 minutes

Remove from the oven, wipe any excess syrup from the necks of the jars, check that the rings and the lids are in place, screw on plastic screwbands tightly, leave for 2-3 minutes then re-tighten, or secure the metal clips. Label and store.

STORAGE

Store bottled fruits in a cool, dark place. A good tip is to smear metal clips with a little oil to prevent rust and to ease opening at a later date. Use jars in rotation.

GIFTS FROM THE COUNTRY RANGE

Home-produced gifts, whether they come from your oven, larder or garden are always greatly treasured and appreciated. You can make all manner of edible presents from biscuits, preserves and pickles to gourmet food ingredients and special sweetmeats, and if you have someone particular in mind it can be personalised like no other commercial gift can. I often pack a 'foodie' friend a basket of culinary vinegars, oils, herbs, preserves and pickles for her experimental cooking and every Christmas give my grandmother a festive hamper bulging with home-made puddings, cakes, chocolates and other favourite things which she eagerly awaits. Simple and inexpensive gifts like a home-made pomander, a bunch or two of dried herbs, a cellophane-wrapped stollen or Christmas cake or a tin of spiced nuts also take on an added value when the recipient knows you have spent valuable time as well as money on the gift. Personally I fall hook, line and sinker for dried flowers so whether I receive a home-dried informal bunch of lavender, a basket of pot-pourri or a terracotta-pot-filled arrangement the gift is received with unrivalled enthusiasm and pleasure.

A FEW IDEAS ON PRESENTATION

- Fill a wicker-style basket for a foodie friend with some of the following: flavoured oils; flavoured vinegars; garlic, thyme and olives preserved in oil; dried herbs; culinary preserves; culinary pickles; chutneys; special bottled fruits and a few welcome small culinary pieces of equipment like a garlic press, mini balloon whisk, Parmesan grater or pizza cutter for example.

- Gift wrap a home-made pomander or two with a hand-made and decorated padded coathanger for the woman who seemingly has everything.

- For the men in your life what could be more welcome than a small basket containing a packet of home-made spiced nuts and seeds with a few nuts in their shell complete with nutcracker or packet of special cigars.

- A jar of special preserves can be given the luxury treatment for a special gift by adding a special or antique preserve spoon. Attach to the jar with a lavish ribbon.

- Home-made pickles have year-round appeal – why not give away a jar or two with a pickling fork – antique shops prove good hunting grounds for them at a reasonable cost.

- If you're calling for Christmas or New Year drinks and don't want to arrive empty handed, wrap up a stollen, tea bread or mini Christmas cake in cellophane and dress with a stunningly-colourful bow.

- The young especially like to experiment with cocktails so why not treat a young adult to a cocktail shaker plus ingredients with some home-made cocktail biscuits and spiced nuts.

- The hostess who entertains regularly will appreciate a home-made table decoration made from home-dried flowers. Try filling miniature clay pots with flowers or flower heads for individual place setting decorations – stud with a scented candle or night light for evening use.

- You don't have to be fervently houseproud to appreciate the benefits of a bowl of pot-pourri in a room. Pack a small basket or bowl for giving and aim to reflect the seasons with the mix of flowerheads, cones, spice sticks and herbal oil from Christmas through spring, to summer and autumn.

- Those with nimble fingers and sewing skills can quickly stitch up a herbal pillow containing home-dried lavender or herbs for a restful night's sleep and its childs play to make a simple lavender sachet to scent a drawer the whole year round.

- First-home dwellers rarely have Christmas tree decorations so why not give them a batch of home-baked cookies threaded with a ribbon loop for their first Christmas tree. So very stylish and smart!

- When its the thought that counts leave a friend, relative or guest who is staying the weekend a basket of fruit and a few home-made biscuits in their room. This is a tip from my late mother-in-law who insisted that you always feel more hungry in someone else's home simply because you don't have free access to the kitchen or larder!

LEMON, ORANGE OR LIME POMANDERS

Carefully stud 1 firm, unblemished lemon, small orange or lime with cloves (you will need about 2 small jars for each fruit pomander), making sure that they are studded carefully together and that no fruit skin shows through. Mix 15 g (½ oz) powdered orris root with 15 g (½ oz) ground cinnamon together on a plate and roll the studded fruit in the mixture to coat thoroughly. Leave on top of or hang above the country range for 3-4 days to dry out, turning occasionally for even drying. To decorate with a hanging ribbon, tie the ribbon in two vertical circles around the pomander, securing very firmly at the top with the loose ends. Tie the loose ribbon ends together to form a loop and finish with a small bow.

DRIED HERBS

I much prefer to use fresh herbs in my cooking for flavouring a dish but it isn't always possible to have them fresh all year round so a few well chosen dried ones are invaluable. All the evergreen varieties like bay, thyme and rosemary can be picked at any time, so they are probably best left alone, but marjoram, sage and mint for example which peak at a certain time in the year are all suitable and useful for drying.

Harvest herbs for drying while relatively young and certainly before they flower – early to mid-summer is the best time. Pick the herbs in mid-morning after the dew has evaporated from them, choosing only choice specimens and discarding any damaged leaves. Large-leaved herbs like sage can be left on or be stripped from their stem, while feathery herbs such as fennel should be left whole.

Drying herbs above the country range cooker is excellent since the heat is dry and constant. Collect the herbs in bunches of the same type and tie to secure. Hang upside-down well above the range and leave for 5-10 days until completely dry. Wrap in muslin or thin paper bags if the area can tend to be dusty but never in polythene since this will cause them to sweat and become mouldy.

Store as bunches, or crumble the leaves from the dried bunches and store in small airtight jars out of direct sunlight.

Alternatively, the herbs can be placed on a baking tray in the Warming Oven and dried here for about 2-3 days then stored as above.

DO REMEMBER WHEN USING DRIED HERBS THAT THEY ARE MORE POTENT IN TERMS OF FLAVOURING POWER THAN THEIR FRESH COUNTERPART. USE ONLY HALF THE RECOMMENDED AMOUNT OF FRESH HERB IN A RECIPE.

DRIED FLOWERS

Flowers dried over the country range look marvellous because their shape and vibrant colours are well preserved. For air drying in this way, flowers are best picked mid-morning when the dew has evaporated but before the sun has become too hot. Arrange in small bunches, about 3 to 4 stems in each bunch and hold together with string or elastic bands – the latter are often better since they contract during the drying process thus keeping a firm hold. Hang above the country range where the air is warm and where there is adequate ventilation. Hang the bunches by their stems, keeping them well apart from one another so that the air can circulate. Most bunches take between 4 days to about 2 weeks to dry although some very fleshy types may take up to 4 weeks. Check every few days and only remove when you feel confident that the bunches are completely dry or they could develop mildew later. For this reason it is not advisable to mix bunches of different flowers since they all take different times to dry which makes the decision process that more difficult. Once dried the flowers can be used immediately or stored. Store in boxes where they are dark, dry and safe from insects or other infestations.

POT-POURRI

For years I bought expensive pot-pourri in small sachets thinking that the process of making my own was difficult – how wrong could I be! The process is simple, effective and most rewarding since you can make different mixtures with different oils for so many different occasions and seasons and, dare I say it, so cheaply if you have access to a garden full of suitable flowers.

To make your own pot-pourri, first you need to combine your chosen fixative with your chosen essential oil and leave them for about 2 days to mature. It is usual to select more than one essential oil for a mixture but each must first be combined with the fixative then later combined for success. This is easiest done in small screw-topped jars. Mix about 175 drops (6 fl oz) of oil with 50 g (2 oz) powdered orris or calamus root to fix. Mix together well, screw on the lid and leave to mature, shaking from time to time. Don't worry if you don't use all of the mixture to begin with – it keeps a very long time. The oils can then be mixed as you please – experiment to your heart's delight with your oils; the aroma must please your nose but there are some suggestions below.

After the maturation process you are ready to mix or 'cook' the mixture. Mix roughly 1 tablespoon of the root and oil mixture to 600 ml (1 pint) dried plant or flower material. Mix well and place in a large jar or bowl and cover tightly with cling film. Store in a dark place for about 2-3 weeks, shaking them at frequent intervals. Use as required.

IDEAS FOR OIL MIXES

YULETIDE CHEER: flower heads with baby pine cones, holly leaves, pine needles, cinnamon sticks, dried orange and lemon peel with a little star anise. Toss with a mixture of fixed pine oil, fixed cinnamon oil, fixed orange oil, fixed rose oil and fixed clove oil.

SUMMER SELECTION: rose buds and petals with dried pansies, lavender and larkspur flowers. Toss with a mixture of fixed lavender oil, fixed allspice oil, fixed rose oil and a few whole cloves.

BATHROOM BLISS: rose buds and petals with lavender, peony petals or heads and pansies. Toss with a mixture of fixed rose oil, fixed lavender oil and fixed orange blossom oil. Add a few small sea shells or pearls if liked.

SLEEPY LAVENDER (for sachets and herbal pillows): lavender flowers with rose petals if liked. Toss with a mixture of fixed lavender oil, rose oil and allspice oil.

INDEX